Phil Leather

THE ANATOMY OF
ADOLESCENCE

THE ANATOMY OF ADOLESCENCE

Young People's Social Attitudes in Britain

ADRIAN FURNHAM
and
BARRIE GUNTER

ROUTLEDGE
London and New York

First published in 1989
by Routledge
11 New Fetter Lane, London EC4P 4EE
29 West 35th Street, New York, NY 10001

© 1989 Adrian Furnham and Barrie Gunter

Phototypeset in 10pt Baskerville by
Mews Photosetting, Beckenham, Kent
Printed and bound in Great Britain by
Mackays of Chatham PLC, Chatham, Kent

British Library Cataloguing in Publication Data
Furnham, Adrian, *1953–*
The anatomy of adolescence: young people's
social attitudes in Britain
1. Great Britain. Adolescents. Attitudes
I. Title II. Gunter, Barrie
305.2'35'0941
ISBN 0-415-00697-X
0-415-00698-8 (pbk.)

Library of Congress Cataloging in Publication Data
also available

CONTENTS

TABLES

INTRODUCTION

This book is a report of the social attitudes of British adolescents. It is not the first of its kind but, we believe, has a number of special features which will be discussed later.

There are many reasons why a comprehensive survey of adolescents' social attitudes is desirable. First, although there are available in the somewhat scattered psychological, sociological, and educational literature a fairly large number of polls, surveys, and reports on social attitudes, they are difficult to compare. Answers are derived from different questions in different contexts and using different sampling methods. Second, there has been a very patchy coverage of research with some topics being consistently and positively examined while others have been ignored. Media-sponsored opinion polls are usually so constrained by budgets, deadlines, and printing space that many interesting and important details are omitted. Third, a detailed account of social attitudes, broken down by age, sex and class, allows not only for comparison within groups at one period of time, but also for the comparison of groups *over time* so that important trends can be detected. Hence the establishment of *Social Trends* and *British Social Attitudes* which attempt to provide a comprehensive and representative account of attitudes at different points in time.

While it may not be disputed that reports on social attitudes are both interesting and important, there remain in the eyes of many sceptics a number of questions about the value of research of this kind. Can social attitudes be measured? How much do people lie? Do social attitudes predict behaviour? What determines social attitudes and beliefs? Given that we can accurately measure social attitudes, how can we go about changing them? Endless, and frequently technical, books have been dedicated to each of these questions and they cannot

1

be covered in any detail here: however, some attempt will be made briefly to answer some of the most frequently posed questions.

CAN SOCIAL ATTITUDES BE MEASURED?

The fact that it is relatively simple to obtain answers to a series of social attitudes questions does not necessarily mean that those attitudes have been correctly or accurately measured. Oppenheim put the point most succinctly in the preface to his well-used text: 'The world is full of well-meaning people who believe that anyone who can write plain English and a modicum of common sense can produce a good questionnaire. This book is not for them' (Oppenheim 1966: iii).

The point being made is that there are numerous traps that people fall into when attempting to devise attitude surveys and questionnaires. Some of the more common problem areas include:

insufficient or inappropriate pilot work to ascertain whether respondents understand questions;
biases in the method of data collection and sampling for non-representative groups;
problems of question sequence or type that lead to lying or socially desirable response sets;
loss of information with much missing data that is impossible to interpret;
ambiguous wording of questions so that respondents do not understand what the researcher had in mind;
response sets independent of content such as extreme responding, yea- or nay-saying.

We have been sensitive to these issues in the selection of question-naires used in this study. Nearly all of the thirty or so measures that were used to make up the final questionnaire had been piloted and successfully used elsewhere in published material. We would not, however, be naive enough to claim that all the questions used in this survey had overcome all the inherent problems with attitude measure-ment. As a result, it is not being argued that each percentage is a precise, exact statement about young Britons' attitudes. There is measurement and sampling error, both of which mean that results are not absolutely correct. Nevertheless, we believe that this book does contain fairly accurately measured social attitudes, within acceptable ranges of error.

HOW MUCH DO PEOPLE LIE?

Critics of surveys argue that, because all self-report is open to various artefacts such as lying, they are practically worthless and we can only really rely on observable behavioural data. There are at least two important issues here. First, there is the extent to which people give inaccurate answers because they choose to present themselves in a positive (or occasionally negative) light or whether they simply cannot give honest answers either because they do not know or because they do not have sufficient insight into their own behaviour. Whereas the latter may be true of surveys measuring personal needs, wants, or motives, it is not so often the case with the social attitude measures found in this book. Second, there is the question of how, when, and why people lie, fake, or present themselves in a socially desirable or occasionally undesirable way. Furnham (1986) has reviewed phenomena such as how questionnaire researchers attempt to catch people who lie, which sorts of questions are most susceptible to lying, and which kinds of people habitually fake. Some questioning techniques have been shown to reduce lying while others increase it. There are a number of reasons to suppose that the survey reported in this book was completed fairly honestly: the respondents were asked to be honest; they filled it out anonymously; there was little or no benefit to be derived from lying; and in many instances it was difficult to determine what was the most socially desirable answer. It would be naive to assume that some of the adolescents did not lie for one reason or another. However, there is little reason to assume that this was either substantial or systematic.

DO SOCIAL ATTITUDES PREDICT BEHAVIOUR?

Most people interested in social attitudes are interested in predicting and changing behaviour and for many there is the naive assumption that attitudes predict behaviour. That is, if we can measure a person's attitude to Frenchmen, a political party's creed, or strawberry jam, then we can accurately infer their behaviour with respect to Frenchmen, their voting habits, or their purchasing and consumption of strawberry jam. The answer, as many people have found, is that overall attitudes are a fairly poor predictor of subsequent behaviour.

However, there are many obvious reasons for this. Consider first the *level of specificity* at which we usually measure attitudes and behaviour. Frequently, attitudes are measured at a very general abstract level and behaviour at a highly specific level. The more the two are in alignment, the better the one predicts the other. Second, consider the problem of *single versus multiple act* measurement. If people are interested in attitudes to women, it is better to look at a series of possible behaviours associated with them. Attitudes are much better predictors when a whole series of behaviours (multiple acts) are taken into account. 'One-shot' measures of behaviour do not give us much information about the relationships between attitudes and behaviour. Third, *situational* factors may strongly influence attitudes as well as behaviours. Where situational pressures are strong, such as at the scene of an accident or in a religious building, people of widely different attitudes may act in a similar way. Fourth, it is possible that a given behaviour might relate to a whole *range of attitudes*. For instance, imagine we are interested in predicting how likely people are to help in accidents, specifically how likely to help a black child knocked over by a motor cyclist. A person might be unfavourably disposed to black people, very positive about children, and very strongly against motor cyclists. It is difficult to know which of these attitudes would best predict behaviour.

Other factors, too, mediate between attitudes and behaviour. However, these factors are known and appear to have a systematic relationship. Thus, rather than despair it may be possible to show a strong relationship depending on how one measures both attitudes and behaviour. For instance, Ajzen and Fishbein have concluded from their extensive research that, 'A person's attitude has a consistently strong relation with his or her behaviour when it is directed at the same target and when it involves the same action' (Ajzen and Fishbein 1977: 912).

WHAT DETERMINES SOCIAL ATTITUDES AND BELIEFS?

This question concerns the origins of social attitudes — where they come from and, to a lesser extent, how they are maintained. How is it that some people are in favour of nuclear disarmament, others against it, while still others do not seem to have an opinion either way? Are these attitudes a result of personality characteristics (authoritarian personalities tend to be against nuclear disarmament); upbringing, education, or social class (working-class, less well-educated people are less likely to approve of disarmament); exposure to or choice of media (tabloid more than quality newspaper readers are likely to be against disarmament); or some other factor? Three important issues mean that the answer to this question (as with the others) is fairly complicated. First of all, factors that lead to the adoption of an attitude often differ from those which maintain it. Second, each set or group of attitudes may be maintained by different factors. Thus, personality factors may relate to racial attitudes, while social-class factors relate to attitudes towards health. Third, these different factors are themselves inter-related and confounded, and hence are difficult to tease apart.

It is the custom in some surveys to break the respondents down by age, sex, and class because these factors are thought to represent major determinants of social attitudes. We have done likewise with the data we present in this book. We also broke the data down by religion and voting preference. In all cases, however, we only report on demographic differences when they were very marked and very clear.

HOW DO WE CHANGE ATTITUDES?

Many agencies are interested in measuring attitudes, often either because they wish to influence how people feel or because those attitudes provide indications of how people behave. Once again this is a complicated issue and there are a number of theoretical approaches to attitude change — learning theory, social judgement theory, consistency theory, functional theories, and so on. Some of the researchers interested in attitude change and communication focus on the characteristics of the *communicator* who is trying to encourage people to change their opinions. Other researchers have focused on the characteristics of the *communication* (message and appeal); still others on the characteristics of the *recipients* (i.e., persuasibility) and others on the frequency of exposure. Thus, we already know something of the factors that can lead to attitude change. Indeed, there is a whole commercial industry built on the study of these factors. But what emerges from all this work is that seemingly straightforward and simple questions often have rather complicated answers.

This book reports on the attitudes of a sample of over 2,000 adolescents from all over the British Isles from the south of England to the north of Scotland, and from Northern Ireland as well as Wales.

Details of the sample are given on pages 12–14 along with the questions they were asked (Tables 1.1 to 1.4). We believe that the data provide a useful and interesting account of the attitudes of young Britons in the 1980s. There are other accounts but they have various limitations. *Young People in the 80s: A Survey*, published by Her Majesty's Stationery Office in 1983, was restricted to around only 600 respondents and was collected in 1982. A study by Simmons and Wade (1984) entitled *I Like to Say What I Think* was collected from a similar number of young people (around 800), at a similar time, 1981, but was restricted to 15-year-olds and the content analysis of ten sample sentences like 'The sort of person I would most like to be like . . .' and 'The best thing about life is . . .'. This book has more in common with the *British Social Attitudes* and the numerous *Gallup Reports* in its scope and numbers of respondents.

We were lucky enough to have the opportunity to gather most (but not all) of the data through the National Association of Youth Clubs and we have Linden Rowley to thank for her help. Some data were gathered in London by students of ours, who also helped in the coding. We also have Lee Drew, Peter Fonagy, and Jeanette Garwood to thank for help with the computing of this huge data set of 800,000 data points.

Finally, we are particularly grateful to Jane De Souza and Philippa Hart for turning our respective scrawls into readable manuscripts.

Adrian Furnham
Barrie Gunter

Bloomsbury
London, 1987

Chapter One

THE ORIGINS OF ATTITUDINAL DEVELOPMENT IN ADOLESCENCE

DEFINING ADOLESCENCE

Adolescence has come to be viewed as a distinct stage of development in most western cultures. As a time period, adolescence may be defined in a number of ways. In contemporary terms, adolescence is identified approximately with the age-range of 11 to 22 years. The traditional age-range of adolescence, 13 to 18 years, is based on the physiological growth and pubertal changes that occur in youth. The contemporary definition reflects increasing social, as well as physical, pressures on young people across a broader age span because of changing social structures.

Thus, in terms of physical development, an individual's adolescent period may be said to have begun at the time that he or she shows the first signs of making the transition to sexual maturity, and to have ended when physical growth has ceased or almost ceased at about the age of 17 or 18. But the period may also be defined in terms of social behaviour, beginning with the increase in interest in the other sex that usually accompanies sexual maturity and ending with the attainment of social and financial independence from parents.

Adolescence occupies a period marked by significant social, personal, and physical changes. This stage of development holds many challenges for the young person, who is required to accept a more mature personal role, be able to think logically, develop a masculine or feminine sex role, and establish good relations with a wide range of other people with whom he or she will interact in society.

Adolescence is also a period when social values and constellations of attitudes and beliefs that accompany them attain complex levels of development. Although many attitudes and values will already have been shaped during the pre-adolescent, childhood years, it is not until adolescence that young people begin to reach stages of cognitive and moral maturity which facilitate the development of advanced, abstract ideas about the world and independent, adult-like modes of thought about important social, political, economic, spiritual, and environmental issues. In this book we will examine the opinions that young people hold of a variety of issues which represent each of these domains.

Youth

The distinction has been drawn by some between adolescence and youth. If adolescence is a long transition, then the period of youth may be thought of as a period of consolidation. For most young people of around 18–22 years, the beginning of the period of youth is marked by the physical transition of leaving home. New issues and tasks emerge during youth — most notably the establishing of intimate relationships.

To a large extent though, the years from 18 to 22 are marked by resolutions or completions of the tasks of adolescence. No real physical changes occur, although final stages of growth and some other pubertal changes may still be continuing for those young people who experienced late onset of puberty. A peak of sexual capacity is reached (especially for males) during this period. The questioning and doubting of adolescence shifts towards achievement of an identity. More importantly, cognitive and moral development continues in most young people, as they become aware of the psychological functioning of individuals, the sociological functioning of individuals, and the sociological functioning of institutions they come into contact with.

Relationships are seen as fundamentally reciprocal, as mutually sharing, and friends are treated with greater tolerance and respect. Such an understanding not only forms the root of forgiveness, it is also one of the underpinnings of intimacy. Many young people establish enduring individual friendships and lasting intimate partnerships during this period. In the research we report in this book, youth as well as adolescence, in terms of the distinct age groups defined above, is represented.

Some social scientists believe that adolescence is universally a time of stress and strife. However, this stress seems not to be a necessary result of physical and emotional maturation. Instead, the strain probably derives from the long interval during which the adolescent feels personally ready to accept independence and social responsibility,

8

but actually remains financially dependent on his/her parents. Western societies have a prolonged period of education and training as a prelude for most jobs or professions. This waiting period, according to some, brings a crisis of identity, during which the young person must struggle to establish his/her own self-concept in the face of social, physical, and emotional changes which challenge him or her.

Adolescence, as a stage of life, is not a universal phenomenon. Historically, society's current view of adolescence as a distinct stage of human development is recent in origin. The Greeks and Romans did not view it as a separate stage, except for that short one- or two-year period when the actual physical change from sexual immaturity to sexual maturity occurred.

The jump straight from childhood into adulthood was typical of classical cultures and of the way of life in the Middle Ages and Renaissance too. Aries (1962) notes that in the 1300s to 1400s boys as young as 5 years old went to school armed, and often had to take off their swords before they were allowed to attend class. Age was not a criterion in deciding what the individual should be taught. Thus, at Caen, France, in 1677, pupils in the primary grade ranged in age from 9 to 17 and those in the highest grade ranged from 12 to 20.

In those days, cultures were not age-graded. For both those who went to school and those who did not, the age of 7 was considered to be the age of adulthood in most of western culture. After 7, a person was legally responsible for his/her crimes and could be hung if the offence warranted it. After this age, children went to work if they were of the working class, and all children were free to take part in all of the activities of adult society. It is only recently that the period of dependence has been extended beyond the age of sexual maturity.

Most historians believe that both our theories of human development and our treatment of children are strongly affected by economic realities. It seems that only a rich culture can afford to allow an extended period of adolescence in which a young person does not earn his or her own living and is dependent upon parents. Adolescence as a social phenomenon is even today not found in all cultures. Within hunting cultures childhood ends by age 8 and within agrarian cultures by age 10 to 12 (Landis 1960). It is only within present-day industrial cultures that the period called adolescence is an extension of childhood dependency.

If adolescence can best be viewed as beginning at sexual maturity and ending at the point when the individual is independent from

9

parental control, it appears that adolescence is lengthening in western culture and in segments of other cultures, too. Sexual maturity is occurring earlier today than previously and dependency on parents continues until a later age.

Muuss (1970) has called attention to what is called the secular trend in human development. This refers to the fact that the growth processes of children and adolescents are accelerating throughout the world. In North America, Europe, and other parts of the world, children and teenagers are taller and heavier than their age counterparts of seventy or even forty years ago. In the United States, for instance, boys, on average, grow to be one inch taller and ten pounds heavier than their fathers. Girls grow to be one-half to one inch taller and two pounds heavier than their mothers.

Puberty also occurs earlier and growth ceases earlier. Studies have compared the interests of junior and senior high-school students in 1935 with those of 1957 students. The latter had greater interest in home, love, marriage and family and greater social awareness than did respondents from the earlier period (Muuss 1970).

Despite more rapid development in adolescence these days, there is a longer period of dependence on parents, economically and socially. Fifty or a hundred years ago adolescents were an asset to the family. The teenage girl was valued as a help to her mother with various domestic chores around the home, while the teenage boy went out to work with his father.

NEW RESEARCH WITH ADOLESCENTS
AND YOUTH IN BRITAIN

This book presents the results of a series of four surveys conducted with adolescent and youth respondents from all parts of the United Kingdom. The respondents fell within the age-range 12 to 22 years and were recruited through the National Association of Youth Clubs as part of an exercise to mark International Youth Year in 1985.

Questionnaires were sent to four separate samples, each of which was spread widely throughout the country. All questionnaires contained a core element of questions and attitude statements which probed for demographic information and several specific topics which comprised political knowledge, racial attitudes, and opinions concerning Britain's involvement and relationships with foreign and developing countries. In addition to this core section, the

Table 1.1 Topics covered by four surveys

Topics common to: All Surveys	Topics unique to each survey			
	Survey One	Survey Two	Survey Three	Survey Four
Demographics: sex, age, social class, number of siblings	Political knowledge	Opinions about inflation and unemployment	Beliefs about school	Beliefs about the environment
	Knowledge of British institutions		Use of new media	Beliefs about health
Living environment: type of community length of residence type of dwelling type of occupancy site of household	Attitudes to nuclear defence	Opinions about getting a job	Smoking and drinking habits	Beliefs about the role of women
	Future problems facing Britain	Beliefs about crime and law enforcement		Beliefs about sex matters
	Perceptions of Trade Unions			Beliefs about marriage
Religious affiliation	Beliefs about the governing of Britain			Beliefs about religious and spiritual matters
Interest in politics	Attitudes to Europe			
Voting preference				
Media habits: television viewing newspaper reading				
Opinions about: foreign countries				
Opinions about: developing countries racial attitudes				

questionnaires carried further sections which dealt with attitudes and beliefs on a variety of other topics which differed from one survey to the next. Thus, respondents in any one survey received a core of questions common to all four surveys and a further battery of items unique to their own sample. The topics covered in each survey are shown in table 1.1.

THE SAMPLES

These surveys were not conducted with nationally representative adolescent and youth samples. However, the NAYC membership from which they were drawn does consist of a demographically well-mixed group with a wide geographic distribution. The demographic profile of the return samples in each survey and of the four samples aggregated are shown in table 1.2. This table indicates that the samples were evenly distributed in terms of sex, age, and number of siblings, but that there were differences between them in terms of their social-class profile. Overall, the samples consisted of more individuals from ABC1 and C2 social categories. In Surveys One and Two, however, ABCs were less well represented than in Surveys Three and Four. In Survey One, the social-class distribution was particularly heavily weighted towards C2s.

Table 1.2 Demographic profiles

	All %	Survey One %	Survey Two %	Survey Three %	Survey Four %
Sex					
Male	52	53	52	56	46
Female	48	47	48	44	54
Age					
10-14	34	39	33	33	30
15-16	35	33	34	36	36
17 and over	31	28	33	31	34
Social class					
ABC1	34	17	29	41	43
C2	50	61	44	50	45
DE	8	16	11	3	6
Unemployed	5	4	8	6	5
Don't know	3	2	8	–	1
Number of siblings					
Five or more	8	7	7	8	8
Three or four	19	19	22	19	19
Two	27	33	23	26	28
One	40	35	43	42	40
None	6	6	6	5	5

In terms of features of respondents' living environment, there were considerable degrees of similarity across samples (table 1.3). Around one in three in each case lived in a city or large town, somewhat more than half lived in a small town or village, while around one in ten lived in the countryside or a rural area. In terms of length of residence, around seven out of ten on average had lived in their current residence for at least ten years, while between one in ten and one in five had lived there for between six and nine years. Relatively few across all four survey samples had moved within the last two years. The distributions across samples for type of dwelling and type of occupancy were also reasonably consistent. Approaching six out of ten lived in a terraced or semi-detached house, while nearly one in three lived in a detached house. Seven out of ten lived in homes which were owned by their parents or guardians.

Table 1.3 Demographic profiles

	All %	Survey One %	Survey Two %	Survey Three %	Survey Four %
Type of community					
city or large town	34	37	33	38	38
small town or village	57	55	57	54	52
countryside/rural area	9	9	10	8	10
Length of residence					
ten years or longer	69	70	66	72	64
six to nine years	14	13	12	13	18
four to five years	6	4	9	5	8
two to three years	7	7	8	5	6
less than two years	4	6	6	3	4
Type of dwelling					
flat/unit	6	4	7	5	6
detached house/cottage	28	31	27	26	29
terrace/semi-detached house	58	60	58	59	55
other	8	5	7	10	10
Type of occupancy					
owner	70	72	70	72	68
rented	30	28	30	28	32

Finally, table 1.4 shows further considerable degrees of similarity across samples in terms of size of household and how many others live with the respondent in each of several age categories. Around eight out of ten respondents lived with three or more other people (adults or children); just over one in ten lived with two others, while less than half the latter number lived with one other person only. Very few claimed to live on their own. About one in ten lived in a household which contained at least one child under 6 years, while seven times as many shared a home with at least one child aged between 6 and 17 years. More than nine out of ten shared a home with at least one person aged over 18 years and in eight out of ten cases there were at least two other people aged over 18. Few respondents, however, lived with someone aged over 60 years.

Table 1.4 People in household

	All %	Survey One %	Survey Two %	Survey Three %	Survey Four %
Number of children aged under 6 years in household					
none	89	87	87	89	89
one	9	11	11	9	9
two	2	2	2	2	2
three or more	<1	0	0	<1	<1
Number of children aged 6-17 years in household					
none	30	29	31	29	31
one	42	43	37	43	43
two	19	20	20	20	20
three or more	9	8	12	8	6
Number of people aged 18 years and over in household					
none	6	4	9	3	8
one	12	11	11	12	12
two	55	55	56	57	50
three or more	27	30	24	28	30
Number of people aged 60 years and over in household					
none	92	94	92	92	92
one	6	4	6	6	5
two	2	2	2	2	3
three or more	0	0	0	0	<1
Total in household, apart from self					
none	1	1	3	<1	2
one	5	4	8	3	8
two	13	12	13	14	13
three or more	81	83	76	82	77

Chapter Two

KNOWLEDGE ABOUT BRITISH POLITICS

In Britain and in many other countries, a great deal more research has been done on young people's political attitudes and beliefs than on their political *knowledge* or their *understanding* of the political process at all levels (Jaros and Grant 1974). This may to some extent be due to the fact that it is assumed that political attitudes are better predictors of political behaviour (i.e., voting) than is political knowledge, though all three are, of course, related. In particular at election times, but also at other times throughout the year, public opinion polls are carried out on a variety of political issues. These rarely focus on adolescent respondents, presumably because until the age of 18 years they cannot vote. But there are, of course, exceptions. For instance, Cochrane and Billig (1982) reported a large survey of over 1,000 British 16-year-olds who seemed rather cynical about the political process. Over half thought that 'politics is a dirty business' and that 'politicians don't care what ordinary people think', while about a third believed that 'real decisions are not made by government, but by the powerful forces which control it'.

Furnham and Gunter (1983) have suggested that the extensive psychological and sociological research into young people's political attitudes can be conveniently divided into four areas: sex differences in socio-political ideology; cross-cultural or cross-national differences in political attitudes and beliefs; the structure of social and political attitudes; and, finally, possible generational and genetic differences in political beliefs and behaviours.

SEX DIFFERENCES

Studies on sex differences in political beliefs in adults and adolescents

15

have revealed fairly consistent findings. Males appear to be more
interested and engaged in politics than females but, when females are
interested in politics, it tends to be local rather than national politics
(Sidanius and Ekehammar 1980; Furnham and Gunter 1983; Furnham
1985a; Ekehammar 1985; Greenstein 1961). Furthermore, a host of
studies have shown that male adolescents have a greater political knowledge and awareness than females (Dowse and Hughes 1971). The
literature on ideological beliefs suggests that females are more conservative than males, though it is unclear why this should be (Furnham
et al. 1985). However, recent research suggests that the opposite is true,
namely that women are less conservative with respect to party choice
and social attitudes (less punitive, racist, and capitalist, and more
egalitarian) but more religious than males (Furnham 1985b). Furthermore, Ekehammar (1985) has also shown that these sex differences
occur within party preference groups such that, although ideological
profiles for males and females are similar within, and different between,
groups, these sex differences remain. In other words, although the
pattern of pro- and anti-attitudes is much the same with respect to
different issues like the United Nations, apartheid, etc., there are consistent differences between males and females. Ekehammar and colleagues
explain the different results of studies in terms of age differences (other
studies had a wider range), education differences (not controlled in
other studies), and the women's liberation movement. According to
these authors, theirs and others' results are not well explained or predicted by biological, Marxist, or socialization theories. Therefore, there
seem to be some noticeable differences between adolescent male and
female's political attitudes, though it is far from clear why they occur.

CROSS-CULTURAL DIFFERENCES

There have also been a number of studies done on adolescents' (mainly
students') political beliefs and attitudes in different countries with
people from different socio-political systems. Oppenheim and Torney
(1974) investigated the social, political, and civic attitudes of over 1,300
10- and 14-year-old children from England, Finland, Italy, the
Netherlands, New Zealand, Sweden, and the United States and found
a number of interesting and predictable differences between them.
They were interested in what the respondents thought about democratic
values and the characteristics of a good citizen. Many studies using
conservatism or F (fascist) scales have yielded interesting results.

Sidanius *et al.* (1979) compared Swedish and Australian psychology students and found the latter were less punitive and had greater ideological consensus and consistency than the former. Later, Furnham (1985a) compared matched groups of British and South African adolescents on a forty-nine-item socio-political test. Not unsurprisingly, the white South Africans were less in favour of equality and sexual freedom and more in favour of religion. Similarly, Furnham (1985b) found white South African students more conservative than British students and tending to be hostile and unsympathetic to victims of social injustice. However, most studies of socio-political attitudes among young people have been concerned with the generality of the factor structure of socio-political scales in different cultures. As Furnham and Gunter (1983) observed,

> Not only are these studies few in number but they suffer numerous methodological weaknesses; arbitrary choice of nations; poor sampling and matching; and perhaps most importantly few attempts to relate social and political attitudes to similarities and differences in the political economic systems of the different nations from which the samples were drawn.

Studies comparing political beliefs and attitudes of adolescents from different countries are extremely interesting but very problematic because of issues of matching samples, ensuring that questions have equivalent meaning in different cultures, etc.

GENERATIONAL DIFFERENCES

Finally, some studies have attempted to uncover genetic or generational differences in political beliefs, especially conservatism. Feather (1977) compared the responses of mothers, fathers, sons, and daughters on the conservatism scale and found that on thirty-five out of the fifty items parents were significantly more conservative than their children, whereas the reverse was true for only two items. These inter-generational differences are due, he argues, to life-span changes (the assumption of greater family and economic responsibility) as well as changes in social trends. Other studies have found significant correlations between parental political interests, attitudes, and viewing patterns and those endorsed by their teenage children (Himmelweit and Swift 1971; Jennings and Niemi 1971). This is a potentially very interesting area of research; namely, what determines young people's political attitudes, behaviours, and beliefs and how they change over time. We know that people probably get more conservative as they get older, but it is certainly not clear what determines how conservative they are in their adolescence.

POLITICAL KNOWLEDGE

Compared to research on political attitudes there have been comparatively few studies of adolescents' knowledge of how the political process works. Dennis and McCrone (1970) found in several countries that, by the age of 10 years, primary-school children could accurately name the country's main political parties and express a preference for one. This was true of 80 per cent of British school children (Himmwelweit *et al.* 1981). But knowing the names of politicians is quite different from knowing how parliamentary democracy or local government works.

One major and important study was carried out by Stradling (1977), who was commissioned by the Hansard Society to produce a reliable estimate of the extent of political knowledge and ignorance in 4,027 British 15- to 16-year-olds which, he believed, could act as a yardstick of political literacy against which to measure the effects of future developments and examine the sources of political information in our own society. He distinguished between *propositional* or *factual* knowledge and *procedural* or *know how* knowledge of politics. He aimed specifically to have a multi-dimensional approach which lessened the risk of underestimating the political awareness of young people. The study attempted to discover the determinants of political awareness and found some evidence of sex differences: boys are more politically knowledgeable than girls (particularly on political office-holders and internal affairs) but no evidence of systematic class differences. Stradling also found fairly strong evidence of schooling effects with grammar-school boys being more knowledgeable than their comprehensive cousins; no evidence of a political education effect; but some evidence of an educational aspiration effect (adolescents who leave school once they have attained the legal minimum age are less likely to fare well on this test). He concluded that

the general lack of political awareness revealed in this report must make depressing reading for anyone who is concerned about the future of our representative democracy and the prospects for greater participation by the public. There is something essentially paradoxical about a democracy in which some eighty to ninety per cent of the future citizens (and the present citizenry) are insufficiently well-informed about local, national and international politics to know not only what is happening but also how they are affected by it and what they can do about it. Most of the political knowledge which they do have is of a rather inert and voyeuristic kind and of little use to them either as political consumers or as political actors. (Stradling 1977: 57)

The authors (Furnham and Gunter 1983) repeated Stradling's study on a smaller population and also attempted to specify various determinants (demographic, media usage, interest) of adolescents' political awareness. They found that the level of adolescents' knowledge about politics was much the same as before. The best predictor of political knowledge was not media usage but expressed interest in political affairs. There was, however, some indication that those who watched more television news tended to have greater political knowledge than those who say they watched less news.

In our youth survey we used the same questions as had been used by Stradling. We did this for a number of reasons — to compare our results with his and also because he had considered a fairly wide range of political issues. We were particularly interested in sex differences and class differences as we suspected, based on other studies, that males as opposed to females and middle-class as opposed to working-class respondents would have a greater and wider knowledge of politics.

KNOWLEDGE OF POLITICAL PARTY POLICIES

Somewhere between one in five (20 per cent) and just over a half (57 per cent) knew the correct answers. In four of the questions, half or more of our respondents got the answer correct. Fifty per cent knew that it was Labour policy to discourage private schools in favour of state schools, while 57 per cent knew it was generally Labour policy to spend less money on defence and more on education and health. Similarly, 51 per cent knew that the Conservative party encouraged tenants of local council houses and flats to buy them and 54 per cent guessed correctly that Conservatives favoured private health and education schemes. More people thought the Labour Party (50 per cent) was in favour of tax cuts than the Conservatives (30 per cent) and just under half (47 per cent) of our sample knew that it was Labour Party policy to nationalize industry so that it was run by the government. Only about one in ten of the respondents recognized the Liberal Party policies of worker-management co-operatives (22 per cent) and wage and price control policies (20 per cent). In other words, the more popular the party, in terms of votes and members in parliament, the more our adolescent sample was able to recognize its political creed.

Table 2.1 Different political party policies

		Conservative %	*Labour* %	*Liberal* %	*SDP* %
1.	Taxes on both people and industries should be cut as soon as possible	<u>30</u>	50	10	10
2.	The Government should take over and run more industries	36	<u>47</u>	13	4
3.	The Government should stop giving help to private schools and create more comprehensive schools	22	<u>50</u>	18	10
4.	Workers and management should co-operate as partners in the running of our industries	22	36	<u>22</u>	20
5.	Council tenants should be encouraged to buy their council houses and flats	<u>51</u>	23	16	10
6.	The amount of public money spent on defence should be cut, and spent instead on such things as education, building new houses, and improving the National Health Service	16	<u>57</u>	17	10
7.	If people want to spend their money on a private bed in a hospital or on educating their children at private schools they should be allowed to do so	<u>54</u>	18	16	12
8.	Inflation can only be checked by passing laws to control wage and price increases	44	26	19	<u>11</u>

Note: Percentages indicate respondents who identified each party as having that policy. Items that are underlined indicate correct answers.

We were particularly interested in sex, class, and age differences, but our statistical analyses showed very few indeed. Only four of twenty-four analyses revealed any significant differences, and these were all in the expected directions, with boys being better at getting the correct answer than girls, older respondents being better than younger ones, and middle-class respondents better than working-class ones. More males (35 per cent) than females (27 per cent) got the answer to question 1 correct and the same result emerged for question 6, where 61 per cent of males got the answer correct compared with 50 per cent of the females. The only substantial age and class differences were both for question 7 which concerned private health and education. Middle-class respondents (77 per cent) tended to get the 'correct' answer more often than did working-class respondents (42 per cent). Also, older respondents, 17 + (44 per cent), got it correct more often than did younger, 15–16-year-olds (30 per cent). However, the fact that there were so few differences suggests that these factors alone do not contribute much to political awareness at this age. Religious beliefs yielded only one significant result with non-believers being more likely to get question 4 correct than believers. Party preference, however, yielded six highly significant results. Respondents who said they would vote Conservative were more likely to get questions 1 (52 per cent vs. 24 per cent) and 7 (66 per cent vs. 50 per cent), while respondents who said they would vote Labour were more likely to get questions 3 (57 per cent vs. 42 per cent) and 6 (76 per cent vs. 49 per cent) correct. On the other hand potential Liberal (and SDP) voters were more likely to get questions 4 (31 per cent vs. 17 per cent) and 8 (30 per cent vs. 12 per cent) correct.

It seems from these results that potential voters are able to spot their chosen parties' policies much more easily than those of any other party. Further, respondents overall were better at identifying the policies of the two main British political parties (Labour and Conservative) than of the more minor or middle-ground parties. Finally, the three questions where over 50 per cent of the sample were correct in their answers concerned not so much industrial or macro-economic politics but public spending and class interests in privatization and nationalization.

Despite the fact that party politics have changed over the past ten years, the results are clearly comparable with those of both previous studies. If anything, the percentage of respondents getting the questions correct was slightly lower than in previous samples but this is no doubt due to the fact that many in the sample were younger (i.e., 10–14) than in the previous studies.

KNOWLEDGE OF POLITICAL LEADERS

We were also interested to know our respondents' knowledge about political leaders. Each respondent was given a multiple choice question with five names (four incorrect, one correct) and two additional options — 'I am not sure' and 'None of these' (see table 2.2).

Table 2.2 Political leaders

Questions	Correct Answer %	Not Sure %
1. Who is the Prime Minister at the moment?	95	4
2. Who is the leader of the Labour Party?	86	8
3. Who is the leader of the Liberal Party?	66	12
4. Who is the leader of the Social Democratic Party?	47	19
5. Who is the Foreign Secretary?	56	19
6. Who is the Chancellor of the Exchequer?	62	19
7. Who is the Home Secretary?	49	19
8. How many Members of Parliament are there in the House of Commons?	20	—

Again, the results are comparable with those of earlier studies, particularly that of Furnham and Gunter (1983), which is an interesting finding given the extended age range of this sample. Nearly 95 per cent knew who the Prime Minister was (Margaret Thatcher), but almost 10 per cent fewer (i.e., 86 per cent) knew who the leader of the Labour Party was (Neil Kinnock). Just under two-thirds (66 per cent) knew the correct answer to the then leader of the Liberal Party (David Steel), but under a half (47 per cent) were able to identify the then leader of the Social Democratic Party (David Owen). Between 50 per cent and 60 per cent of this sample could identify the Foreign Secretary at the time (Sir Geoffrey Howe), the Chancellor of the Exchequer (Nigel Lawson), and the Home Secretary (Leon Brittan). Yet only one in five knew the correct number of MPs — that is, 635 (22 per cent thought that there were 140, and 25 per cent 395 MPs). Overall, though, it seems that the respondents had a pretty good idea who the major politicians were.

Only three (12 per cent) out of the twenty-four sex, age, and class chi-squared analyses yielded significant results. More males than females knew who the Chancellor of the Exchequer was (69 per cent vs. 52 per cent); older respondents (i.e., 17 + years) were more likely than younger to know the number of MPs (35 per cent vs. 14 per cent) and middle-class respondents had a better knowledge than working-class respondents of MP numbers (31 per cent vs. 17 per cent). There were no differences due to religious belief and only two voting preference differences. Potential Liberal voters were more likely to know who the leader of the Liberal Party was than were those who would have voted for other parties, and also how many MPs sat in the House of Commons (78 per cent vs. 59 per cent).

These are interesting results that may change with various phenomena like general elections, scandals, or cabinet changes. In other words, it is likely that respondents' knowledge about politicians is closely related to how frequently they appear on the media.

PARLIAMENTARY AND LOCAL
POLITICAL KNOWLEDGE

Again, the pattern of correct responses to these true-false questions was not dissimilar to that of either two previous studies using these items.

Table 2.3 Parliamentary and local political knowledge

		True %	False %	Not Sure %
1.	A backbench MP is any Member of Parliament who is not a Government Minister	47	_19_	34
2.	The political party which gets most votes at the general election always forms the government	48	_32_	20
3.	A general election must be held at least every four years in this country	69	_19_	12
4.	Anyone over the age of 18 can become a Member of Parliament	48	_27_	25
5.	Before an MP can become a Government Minister for a particular subject (e.g. industry), he or she must have some previous experience in the subject	38	_28_	34
6.	Members of Parliament do not have to live in the constituencies which they represent	_42_	27	31
7.	The Prime Minister is the only person who can choose when to call a general election	_33_	44	23
8.	Local councillors have the right to change laws which have been passed by parliament	10	_59_	31
9.	Local councillors have to stand for election every three years	_39_	19	42

Note: Options that are underlined are the correct answers.

23

Furthermore, the adolescents' knowledge was not particularly impressive as fewer than a *third* of the sample were correct in their answers to only *two-thirds* of the questions (questions 1,2,3,4,5,7) and on only one question did more than half of the sample get the answer correct. It is, however, true to point out that these were fairly difficult (possibly perceived to be trick) questions and that a representative adult sample may not do much better. There were *no* age, class, religious belief, or vote preference differences and only one sex difference, suggesting that none of these demographic factors related directly to political knowledge of this type.

It is interesting to note which of the questions were correctly answered and which not. Most of the respondents knew that local politicians cannot overrule parliamentary rules. About 40 per cent knew that an MP does not have to live in his or her constituency. But less than one in five (i.e., under 20 per cent) knew that a general election need not be held every four years or that a backbench MP is not just any member of parliament who is not a government member.

Two further things need to be said about these results. First, that there is no evidence to suggest that an enfranchised adult population actually knows significantly more than our respondents. Second, their lack of knowledge may, in fact, have little or nothing to do with their ability to undestand or take part in parliamentary democracy.

PUBLIC SERVICES

Compared with their knowledge of parliamentary and council affairs, our respondents appeared to be relatively well informed as to who was responsible for public services. Table 2.4 shows how closely the results of this study accord with those of Stradling (1977). Two-thirds of the sample were correct for three questions (3, 4, and 7) and more than half were correct in all questions. Approximately 10 per cent claimed not to know the answers to each question, though some took a guess by ticking both an answer and 'don't know'. The question most respondents knew the answer to (responsible for parks and swimming baths) may well reflect their interests and experience. Similarly, as they are unlikely to pay water 'bills', it is not surprising that so few (comparatively) know about the water supply.

Table 2.4 Knowledge of the public services

Who is responsible for the following services?	The Government %	Local Council %	Regional Board %	Don't Know %
1. The water supply	10	23	<u>56</u>	11
2. Social Security	<u>65</u>	19	6	10
3. Refuse Collection	8	<u>71</u>	9	12
4. Parks and swimming pools	5	<u>75</u>	13	7
5. Electricity supply	18	11	<u>61</u>	10
6. Providing houses	25	<u>62</u>	4	9
7. Hospitals and clinics	<u>67</u>	13	11	9

Note: Items that are underlined are the correct answers.

CONCLUDING REMARKS

We are able to look at two major issues here. The first was to examine political knowledge levels among young people in Britain using political questions originally studied by Stradling (1977), ten years after his investigation. Results from both studies were highly similar even though British politics have changed considerably in the past ten years with the emergence of a strong third party alliance. Nevertheless, the pattern of knowledge and ignorance has remained much the same.

Young people in our sample appeared to be most familiar with local politics — specifically knowledgeable about public services, where they could accurately distinguish between governmental, local council, and regional board responsibilities. They were also well informed about political leaders, especially the Prime Minister and Opposition leader. Their greatest area of ignorance concerned party political and parliamentary knowledge where their knowledge was patchy. There were, for instance, quite large proportions of 'not sure' answers to questions on parliamentary knowledge, as well as ignorance of Liberal Party policy. In other words, although they knew who politicians were, they did not have a very comprehensive or well-informed picture of how the political system actually works. The results tend to suggest that adolescents' political knowledge is limited to areas that they have probably had most experience of, or been most exposed to.

In Stradling's original report he provided evidence that not all adults had a much wider knowledge of political practices than the adolescent sample. Yet he concluded:

> In fact it is apparent that they [his sample] lack much of the
> kind of basic information which the political consumer needs if
> he is to understand decisions and actions which affect him and
> if he is to make political choices between actions, policies,
> parties or candidates. One of the most disturbing findings . . .
> is their ignorance of where the political parties stand on the
> main issue of the day. (Stradling 1977: 23)

It should be pointed out that the majority of respondents in our study
had between two and five years before they were eligible to vote and
it is possible (though unlikely) that their knowledge would increase
over this period (Furnham and Lewis 1986).

There seems to be little evidence of any major changes over the
last ten years in young people's understanding or knowledge of politics.
Indeed, there is no real reason to suppose that any major change has
occurred. This does nothing to lessen concern about a politically
ignorant and ill-informed electorate. Blumler (1974) suggested that
ignorant electors put pressure on governments to adopt ill-conceived
and undesirable policies. Many government policies can only be
effective if the public understands the necessity for them, and a
politically ignorant public is all too easily manipulated. Our results
suggest that more attention perhaps needs to be paid to political education in schools so as to produce a more politically literate population.
However, this education would need to cover many other, perhaps
more important questions first rather than those put to our respondents
regarding their knowledge of politics.

We are also interested in age, sex, and class differences in political
knowledge. Stradling (1977) found some evidence of sex differences
(boys got about one and a half times as many answers correct as girls);
a small but not significant class effect (middle-class knew more than
working-class respondents); a notable type of school effect (with
grammar-school children knowing more than secondary-modern
children); a small educational factor (those leaving at 18 knowing more
than those intending to leave at 16); and a small political education
factor (those who had had lessons in politics knew more). Of course,
it should be pointed out that some four of these variables are confounded. For instance, middle-class children are more likely to attend
grammar schools, stay on until they are 18 years old, and have political
education. Furnham and Gunter (1983) provided modest evidence for
sex and class differences but found that interest in politics was the

strongest determinant of all of political knowledge. The present survey produced few sex and class differences, and also, surprisingly, few age differences. There was evidence that potential voters for a particular party were better able to recognize their party's political agenda than that of another party.

Why is it then that there is fairly strong evidence for sex differences in socio-political beliefs and attitudes, but very little evidence of sex differences in political knowledge? There could be at least two explanations. First, attitudes and knowledge are unrelated and not dependent on one another. Second, it may be that socio-political beliefs and attitudes precede understanding of the workings of the political system. Furnham and Lewis (1986) have found that class attitudes (to money and related issues) are determined before adolescence, but that it is not until early adulthood when people have some conception of macro-sociological and economic forces that they can fully understand the economic process. It may well be that political knowledge and understanding are not the same in that the latter is not fully comprehended until early adulthood, while the former is acquired much earlier.

However, this begs the question as to what determines political knowledge (and attitudes) if not the classic demographic variables considered earlier. The answer may well be partly tautological, as Furnham and Gunter (1983) have already indicated. Those young people who, for whatever reason, are interested in politics, expose themselves to more political coverage on the media and hence learn more about it. It is not surprising that the sample's knowledge was best in terms of individual politicians as it is frequently through individual personalities that television, in particular, reports political events. What we need to know is what makes children interested in politics in the first place, and whether (indeed how) their political interests lead to increased political knowledge and behaviour such as voting preference, standing for election, or canvassing.

Chapter Three

THE GOVERNING OF BRITAIN

What do young Britons think about the way in which their country is governed? What do they think about the apparently unsolvable and intractable problem of Northern Ireland? Do they think major British institutions are well run? What is their attitude to nuclear defence, the problems facing Britain, and the trade unions? These are questions frequently posed to adults but rarely to adolescents.

Nearly all these questions are political in the wider sense of the word. However, a great deal has been written about political socialization and children's understanding of politics. Many researchers have attempted to specify what factors or agents are important in the development of young people's political knowledge, beliefs, and behaviours. Langton (1969) has provided a fairly standard list which includes:

the *family* — it has been suggested that the family structure, particularly the authority/decision-making structure and the power relations between parents, as well as the separate and combined interests and influences of the mother and father, are powerful and important socializing agents.

the *school* — this provides both a formal environment with a curriculum that may specifically or tangentially cover political issues and an informal environment that socializes various political beliefs and behaviours;

the *peer group* — friends, neighbours, and acquaintances are encountered in schools, clubs, and the neighbourhood, all of whom may influence political thinking;

other *agencies* — this includes the media, the church, and various social groups who attempt to inculcate specific ideologies which have political significance.

It is precisely because these different factors influence adolescents' political thinking simultaneously that it is so difficult to determine *which* factor has most effect on *which* attitude or behaviour and *when*.

Stevens has argued that children start to construct concepts about politics at about the age of 7 and that subsequently these develop through specific stages closely resembling Piaget's model of cognitive growth. Even at 7 years old children have some basic political beliefs, ideas, and vocabulary, and by 9 some have a basic grasp of concepts like democracy, leadership, and accountability of government. As Stevens observes, 'Some of these nine-year-olds were instinctive social-contract theorists: Hobbes and Rousseau were not only resuscitated but re-invented, and when ideas for re-thinking social arrangements were produced, they were justified with considerable feeling and no lack of convincing rhetoric' (Stevens 1982: 168). Interestingly, Stevens is critical of previous work on the influence of the family because it implies a passive, receptive child who simply absorbs the parentally transmitted facts, values, and affiliations. Rather, the influence of the family is to provide language structures through which family groups collectively interpret information and events from the outside world. The specific contribution of early schooling, on the other hand, is to create a strong attachment to the idea of law and order as expressed in rule-keeping. It is the role of television that appears to be very important for young children as can be observed in their use of idiomatic television language. Television appears to stimulate interest and curiosity and provides starting-points for further discussion; it provides many items of discrete knowledge but not necessarily conceptual understanding.

However, from their analysis of 12,000 7–13-year-old American children, Hess and Torney have concluded that

> the school apparently plays the largest part in teaching attitudes, conceptions, and beliefs about the operation of the political system. While it may be argued that the family contributes much to the socialisation that goes into basic loyalty to country, the school gives content, information and concepts which expand and elaborate these early feelings of attachment. (Hess and Torney 1967: 217)

And later, 'It is our conclusion from these data that the school stands out as the central, salient and dominant force in the political socialisation of the young child' (ibid.: 219). Hess and Torney also pointed out developmental patterns in the rate and sequence of the acquisition of political knowledge and beliefs. There are individual differences that affect the acquisition of political attitudes and behaviour. They found that sex differences in political attitudes and activities were not large but consistent over age.

The child's intelligence, however, appeared to be an important mediating influence in the acquisition of political behaviour, in that high intelligence tends to accelerate the process of political socialization. Thus, children of high intelligence are found to be more active, more likely to discuss political matters, and more interested in current events. In addition, they have a greater sense of the importance of voting and citizen participation. In sum, intelligence is associated with greater involvement in political affairs. Social-class differences are less important but show a tendency for low-status children to feel less efficacious in dealing with the political system than do children from high-status homes.

In accepting all of this, one might expect to find sex, age, and class differences in adolescents' political beliefs. Another interesting question concerns the differences between adolescent and adult opinions on the governing of Britain. Of the many possible topics to examine seven were chosen.

Northern Ireland

Since the 1960s and the beginning of the 'troubles', the topic of Northern Ireland has rarely been out of the British media. It is, furthermore, a topic that frequently crops up when 'outsiders' or 'foreigners' consider British politics. As a result, there have been numerous surveys and polls. In their 1984 report on *British Social Attitudes*, Jowell and Airey asked 1,761 British adults whether Northern Ireland should remain part of the United Kingdom or reunify with Ireland. Just over a quarter (28 per cent) recommended remaining in the United Kingdom and about 60 per cent reunification, though it was established that Conservatives were more in favour of remaining part of the UK than people who supported other political parties. They also asked about troop withdrawals. Overall, nearly 60 per cent supported withdrawal while a third (33 per cent) opposed it.

However, there was fairly strong party polarization on this issue — among the third who opposed withdrawal were about a quarter of Labour supporters and half of the Conservatives.

British institutions

As children get older they tend to become more aware of the nature and functioning of institutions such as banks, the civil service, trade unions, etc. By and large, polls and surveys have been more concerned with some of these — such as the police and the trade unions — than others. Jowell and Airey (1984) asked people how well or badly run they thought were a dozen major British institutions. Only four were rated as well run by over half the sample: banks (85 per cent); police (72 per cent); independent television and radio (69 per cent) and the BBC (67 per cent), while three were rated by only a third of the respondents as well run: local government (33 per cent); trade unions (27 per cent); and nationalized industries (20 per cent). Overall about half felt that the press (49 per cent); the National Health Service (49 per cent); and prisons were well run, and manufacturing industry (47 per cent) and the civil service (48 per cent) were *not* well run. Perhaps the best known British 'institution', the monarchy, always attracts a great deal of attention and comment. In their adult study Jowell and Airey found 65 per cent thought it *very* important and 21 per cent *quite* important that Britain continues to have a monarchy. We were interested in both of these issues.

Nuclear defence

A topic that seems to attract more and more interest and concern is that of nuclear weapons, and to a lesser extent nuclear power. We were interested in whether adolescents thought nuclear weapons made Britain a safer or less safe place to live and also whether British nuclear policy should be based on the retention or the renunciation of nuclear weapons. In all, 60 per cent of the adults (Jowell and Airey 1984) felt nuclear weapons made Britain safer while 28 per cent said less safe. There were, as one might predict, strong party-allegiance differences with the majority of Conservatives feeling nuclear missiles made Britain safer and only about half Labour party supporters feeling likewise. Thus, it was not surprising that 77 per cent of adults felt that Britain should keep its nuclear arms and only 19 per cent thought it should get rid of them. Predictably, Conservatives were more in favour of keeping the weapons than Labour party supporters. Further, Jowell and Airey found females generally more hostile towards nuclear weapons on British soil than are men. Whereas males from 18 to over 55 were more or less evenly divided on American nuclear weapons in Britain, young and middle-aged women are divided almost 2:1 against.

Overall, opinion-poll studies on British attitudes appear to be fairly consistent. For instance, Webb and Wybrow (1981) found that, in 1980, 67 per cent of people were in favour of keeping nuclear weapons while only 17 per cent were against them. Our quest was to investigate current adolescent views on these issues.

Expectations of problems facing Britain

One important aspect of how a country is governed is how institutions and political processes can be relied upon to prevent and militate against major catastrophic changes. Jowell and Airey (1984) asked their adult population to make predictions about political terrorism, riots and civil disturbance, a world war involving Britain and Europe, a serious accident at a nuclear power station, police incapacity. None of the above scenarios was thought of as *very* likely to occur, though 17 per cent thought the city police would find it impossible to protect personal safety. But about a third or over of the respondents thought it *quite* likely that acts of political terrorism would be common (38 per cent), riots and civil disturbances would be common (41 per cent), there would be a serious nuclear power station accident (32 per cent) and city police would find it impossible to protect personal safety. Only 23 per cent thought it likely that there would be a world war involving Britain and Europe, and even fewer (7 per cent) that the British government would be overthrown by revolution.

Overall, the adults appeared sanguine about major problems facing the country. Data on the same questions collected in 1979, 1980, and 1983 showed interesting trends. People tended to be more optimistic (i.e., finding them less likely) about nuclear accidents and revolution but more pessimistic about political terrorism and safety on the streets. A central question in our study was how do these views compare with those of our adolescent population.

Trade unions

A topic that consistently exercises political pollsters is the trade unions. Numerous polls have looked at such things as general attitudes to the trade unions, beliefs about how good particular unions are, trade union reform, etc. (Furnham 1984a). However, the issue that has perhaps been most consistently debated is the influence of the trade unions. For instance, Jowell and Airey (1984) found that 59 per cent of their adult sample believed the trade unions had too much influence and about a third (34 per cent) about the right amount. Actual trade union membership split people evenly as to whether unions had too much (48 per cent) or about the right amount (44 per cent) of influence but very few supported the proposition that unions had too little influence.

Law observance

Although there are a host of questions which could be asked about the law (see chapter 4), we were particularly interested in two issues — political law-breaking and the death penalty. Asked by Jowell and Airey (1984) if they would obey the law without exception, 53 per cent of the respondents said always, while 46 per cent said they would follow their conscience even if it meant breaking the law. This question showed dramatic sex and age differences. Men, from all age groups, were more likely to break the law than women, and older people (55 + versus 18–34 years old) were, in their own estimation, both less likely to break the law and more likely to agree that it should be obeyed 'without exception'.

Overall, 30 per cent said that there were circumstances in which they thought they might break a law they were opposed to while 60 per cent said no. Despite the fact that the death penalty is not enforced in Britain except for certain specific acts (i.e., treason), the polls consistently revealed that the majority of the population are in favour of it. We were particularly interested in the extent to which young people were in favour of the death penalty for murder as well as murder of a policeman or terrorist murder.

The governing of Britain

Finally, we were interested in adolescents' democratic and citizenship values. We used the thirty questions devised by Oppenheim and

Torney (1974) in their study of civic education in seven countries. They found those thirty items tapped four basic dimensions — authoritarianism, tolerance and civil liberties, personal efficacy, and women's rights. As this questionnaire covered so many aspects of the issues which we were concerned with, we decided to use it in this study.

NORTHERN IRELAND

We asked two questions about Northern Ireland. The first concerned the issue of reunification and the second that of troop withdrawal (see table 3.1) Of those who expressed a preference, there was almost exactly an even split between those who recommended that Northern Ireland remain part of the United Kingdom and those who recommended reunification with the south. This was quite unlike the adult sample from the 1984 *British Social Attitudes* survey where only a quarter were in favour of Northern Ireland remaining part of the UK. However, there were interesting and noticeable sex and age differences. Males were less in favour of the status quo (45 per cent) and more in favour of reunification (55 per cent), whereas it was precisely the opposite case with females. There was a similar striking age difference — more younger respondents were broadly in favour of the status quo (57 per cent) while fewer older respondents (35 per cent) favoured the position and conversely few younger respondents (43 per cent) and more older respondents (65 per cent) favoured reunification.

The results of the second question were, however, more similar to those of adults with about two-thirds (67 per cent) supporting troop withdrawal and a third (33 per cent) opposing it. Here again, however, there were age and sex differences. Males were more in favour of withdrawal (70 per cent) than females (63 per cent), while younger children were less in favour of the status quo (namely the maintenance of troops) (70 per cent) and older respondents were less in favour of maintenance of troops (60 per cent). These differences may reflect the fact that males tend to be more radical in their political beliefs than females, particularly with respect to external events, and that younger adolescents tend to be more inherently conservative than older adolescents.

Table 3.1 Opinions about Northern Ireland

Do you think the long-term policy for Northern Ireland should be for it to remain part of the United Kingdom, or to reunify with the rest of Ireland?

	All %	Sex Male %	Female %	10-14 %	Age 15-16 %	17 + %
Remain in the UK	49	45	55	57	54	35
Reunification	51	55	45	43	46	65

Some people think that government policy towards Northern Ireland should include a complete withdrawal of British troops. Would you personally support or oppose such a policy? Strongly or a little?

	All %	Sex Male %	Female %	10-14 %	Age 15-16 %	17 + %
Strongly support	26	32	17	25	22	23
Support a little	41	38	46	45	40	47
Oppose a little	18	12	25	17	21	13
Oppose strongly	15	18	12	13	17	17

BRITISH INSTITUTIONS

We were interested in two basic issues. First, how well or badly run did our adolescents think a dozen major British institutions were; and their attitude to the monarchy (see table 3.2). The results were fairly similar to those other surveys had revealed of adults, except that adolescents were more generous, seeing these institutions, by and large, in a more favourable light. Thus, the top four were the same: banks (91 per cent); independent television and radio (76 per cent); the police (74 per cent) and the BBC (69 per cent) were thought to be well run. The bottom four were the National Health Service (42 per cent); prisons (42 per cent); local government (41 per cent); and the trade unions (36 per cent). Perhaps the most striking difference between adults and adolescents was in their attitudes to the nationalized industries: only 20 per cent of the former thought they were well run compared to 51 per cent of the latter.

We also found consistent evidence of sex differences. Females more than males tended to think that nearly all institutions, especially banks, police, and the BBC, were better run, with the exception of the press and the prisons which they thought less well run. There were no significant differences with respect to independent TV and radio, the National Health Service and the trade unions.

Overall, adolescents felt the monarchy less important than did adults. Only 69 per cent of adolescents compared to 87 per cent of adults thought it was important for Britain to continue to have a monarchy. Similarly, whereas 10 per cent of our adolescent sample were in favour of abolishing the monarchy, only 3 per cent of the adult sample expressed this view (Jowell and Airey 1984). Once again there were sex differences. Females were much more in favour of the monarchy (79 per cent) than males (62 per cent) and many fewer (4 per cent) believed it should be abolished compared to males (15 per cent). Overall, then, it seems that British adolescents are fairly confident that major British institutions are well run with perhaps the major exceptions of the trade unions and local government.

Table 3.2 Opinions about British institutions

Listed are some of Britain's institutions. From what you know or have heard about each one can you say whether, on the whole, you think it is well run or not well run?

		Well Run			Not Well Run	
	Total %	Male %	Female %	Total %	Male %	Female %
Banks	91	88	94	9	12	7
The police	74	68	82	26	32	18
Independent TV and radio	76	76	75	24	24	25
The BBC	69	68	72	31	32	28
The press	50	52	48	50	48	52
The National Health Service	42	44	42	58	56	58
Prisons	42	45	40	57	55	60
Manufacturing industry	54	52	58	46	48	42
The Civil Service	56	55	58	45	48	42
Local government	41	39	43	59	61	57
The trade unions	36	36	35	64	64	65
Nationalized industries	51	53	49	49	47	51

How about the Monarchy or the Royal Family in Britain? How important or unimportant do you think it is for Britain to continue to have a Monarchy?

	All %	Male %	Female %
Very important	37	35	40
Quite important	32	27	39
Not very important	17	19	13
Not at all important	4	4	4
Should be abolished	10	15	4

NUCLEAR DEFENCE

The results from our three questions on this issue show interesting comparisons with the adult population and some striking sex differences. When asked do you think that the siting of American nuclear missiles in Britain makes Britain a safer or less safe place to live, far more of our adolescents (68 per cent) compared to adults from the 1984 British Social Attitudes survey (48 per cent) thought Britain was a *less safe* place to live because of the siting of American nuclear missiles in the country. Similarly, when asked do you think that having our own independent nuclear missiles makes Britain a safer or a less safe place to live, many more adolescents (49 per cent) compared to adults (28 per cent) thought Britain *less safe* by having its own independent nuclear missiles, though it should be admitted that 51 per cent of adolescents thought the missiles made Britain more safe.

We also asked our respondents if Britain should get rid of its nuclear weapons or try to persuade others to do so first. Whereas 39 per cent of adolescents believed we should get rid of our (Britain's) nuclear weapons, only 19 per cent of the adult sample thought so. Similarly 42 per cent of adolescents wanted to keep the nuclear weapons compared to 77 per cent of the adults. This is in keeping with Jowell and Airey's (1984) findings that hostility to nuclear weapons in general comes from the young and decreases with age. However, contrary to their findings, when there was a significant sex difference it showed that females were more pro-nuclear weapons in the sense of the status quo than males. This appears to be contrary to women's movements which protest against nuclear weapons.

EXPECTATIONS OF PROBLEMS FACING BRITAIN

If one simply considers those problems listed in table 3.3 that 50 per cent or more think likely or unlikely to occur, it seems British adolescents are fairly pessimistic about the future. About 80 per cent expect to see more acts of political terrorism, 64 per cent more city riots and civil disturbance, but 68 per cent believe a world war involving Britain and Europe is likely as is the overthrow of the British government by revolution (75 per cent). Over half (57 per cent) believe a serious nuclear accident in Britain likely; but just under half (49 per cent) believe the police in our cities will be able to protect personal safety. The rank order of the probability of occurrence is almost identical for adolescents and adults but the likelihood is seen as greater by the former for all events, particularly political terrorism. It seems, then, that young people anticipate fairly serious problems ahead for their country particularly with respect to civil disturbance.

Table 3.3 Future problems facing Britain

Here is a list of predictions about problems that Britain might face. For each one, please say how likely or unlikely you think it is to come true in Britain within the next ten years.

	Very likely %	*Quite likely* %	*Not very likely* %	*Not at all likely* %
Acts of political terrorism in Britain will be more common events	30	50	18	2
Riots and civil disturbance in our cities will be common events	21	43	31	5
There will be a world war involving Britain and Europe	11	21	48	20
There will be a serious accident at a British nuclear power station	17	40	33	10
The police in our cities will find it impossible to protect our personal safety on the streets	16	35	40	9
The Government in Britain will be overthrown by revolution	11	14	40	35

TRADE UNIONS

We asked only two questions about trade unions as young people are not likely to have much experience of them. These concerned perceptions of how much influence trade unions have, and whether they are thought to have too much influence or not. Just over a quarter (26 per cent) thought trade unions had a *great deal* of influence on the lives of people in Britain and 36 per cent quite a bit of influence, 29 per cent some influence, and 9 per cent not much influence. This compares well with the adult sample where more than two-thirds thought that unions had a great deal or quite a bit of influence, the remainder saying 'some influence', but hardly anyone saying 'not much'. However, whereas 42 per cent of the adolescents thought the unions had too much and 12 per cent too little influence, 59 per cent of the adults thought too much, 46 per cent about the right amount, and 5 per cent too little. Overall, these results tend to indicate that the young people are not as distrustful of the unions as adults.

LAW OBSERVANCE

We began by asking adolescents if in general they felt that people should obey the law without exception, or if there are exceptional occasions on which people should follow their consciences even if it means breaking the law. Whereas 53 per cent of adults (Jowell and Airey 1984) said that they would obey the law without exception, only 36 per cent of adolescents agreed that they would. Similarly, while 46 per cent of adults said they would occasionally break the law to follow their conscience, nearly two-thirds (64 per cent) of the adolescents claimed they would on occasion break the law. Then we asked, are there any circumstances in which you might break a law to which you were very strongly opposed? Whereas less than a third of adults (30 per cent) thought there might be circumstances where they would break the law, over half (51 per cent) of the adolescents could think of examples. Predictably perhaps, nearly one in three of the adolescents (29 per cent) claimed that they did not know the answer to the question.

Then, finally, we asked whether they were in favour of or against the death penalty in various cases. Overall, the adolescent sample were in favour of the death penalty for murder — nearly three-quarters (73 per cent) were in favour of executing terrorist murders, two-thirds (66 per cent) in favour of the death penalty for general murders, and slightly fewer (62 per cent) in favour of executing those who murdered policemen.

As one may expect, the adolescents in general appeared to be more willing to break the law than adults. Paradoxically, however, they are very conservative in their reactions to murderers.

THE GOVERNING OF BRITAIN

The results of the thirty questions about British children's civic attitudes are given in table 3.4. These will be discussed briefly in sequence, though it should be borne in mind that there are established specific dimensions underlying these items. More adolescents are in favour (55 per cent) than against (28 per cent) newspapers being able to print anything except military secrets, though there is a noticeable sex difference. Females are less in favour of this than males (50 per cent vs. 56 per cent), indicating some approval of secrecy and of a censored or partly censored press.

Table 3.4 The governing of Britain

Here are some things that have been said about the way our nation should be governed. You may agree with some of them and disagree with others; sometimes you will agree or disagree strongly; at other times you will feel uncertain or have no opinion. Please look at each statement, and then put a tick (✔) in one of the columns beside it to show how you feel about it.

	Agree %	Neither %	Disagree %
Newspapers and magazines should be allowed to print anything they want except military secrets	55	17	28
Women should stand for election and take part in the government much in the same way as men do	80	14	6
No matter what a person's colour, religion or nationality, if s/he is qualified for a job s/he should get it	77	15	8
The government cares a lot about what we all think of any new laws	29	32	39
People should be allowed to come together whenever they like	74	19	7
Swimming pools should admit people of all races and nationalities to swim together in the same pool	76	12	12
Citizens must always be free to criticize the government	81	15	4
Hotels are right in refusing to admit people of certain races or nationalities	24	16	60
People who disagree with the government should be allowed to meet and hold public protests	64	25	11
Regular elections in our nation are necessary	73	24	3
Women should have the same rights as men in every way	73	18	9
People of certain races or religions should be kept out of important positions in our nation	31	25	44
Women should stay out of politics	14	17	69

	Agree %	Neither %	Disagree %
Government decisions are like the weather; there is nothing people can do about them	45	27	28
There are some big powerful men in the government who are running the whole nation and they do not care about the opinions of ordinary people	52	32	16
Most women do not need the right to vote	15	24	61
The government is doing its best to find out what ordinary people want	30	24	46
When something is wrong it is better to complain to the authorities about it than to keep quiet	74	21	5
It is good for a government to be frequently criticized	79	19	2
The government does not try to understand us	50	28	22
Most politicians are too selfish to care about ordinary people	46	31	23
War is sometimes the only way in which a nation can save its self-respect	27	22	51
The people in power know best	15	17	68
If another nation does not agree with us, we should sometimes fight them	17	22	61
So many people vote in a general election that when I grow up it will not matter whether I vote or not	23	24	53
Talking things over with another nation is better than fighting	77	15	8
It is wrong to criticize our government	15	24	61
I don't really care what happens to others, so long as I am all right	17	20	63
Our nation has its faults just like other nations	82	12	6
People should not criticize the government, it only interrupts the government's work	14	25	61

Predictably, there was a sex difference on the item about women standing for parliament in which 80 per cent agreed and only 6 per cent disagreed. In all, 81 per cent of females approved and none were against, while 72 per cent of males agreed and 8 per cent were against. There was also a dramatic sex difference on the item about job discrimination in which over three-quarters (77 per cent) believed that neither colour, religion, nor nationality should prevent a person getting a job. Females agreed more frequently than males (83 per cent vs. 70 per cent) and disagreed less frequently (4 per cent vs. 13 per cent), which is consistent with the literature on sex differences in political beliefs (see chapter 2).

The sample were undecided about the item which stated that the government cares a lot about what we think of any new laws, with slightly more disagreeing than agreeing (39 per cent vs. 29 per cent) but 32 per cent undecided. Yet three-quarters (74 per cent) approved the right of free assembly with few dissenting (7 per cent) and no sex differences. Much the same number (76 per cent) agreed that swimming pools should admit people of all races and nationalities. Once again there was a sex difference, with females being more liberal by agreeing more (80 per cent) than males (75 per cent).

Curiously, although there was overall agreement (81 per cent) that citizens must always be free to criticize the government, fewer females (77 per cent) than males (83 per cent) agreed with this. But there were no sex differences with regard to the item on hotels refusing to admit people of certain races or nationalities where 60 per cent disagreed and only a quarter (24 per cent) agreed.

Again, females were more conservative on the issue of public protest meetings with 60 per cent being in favour as opposed to 66 per cent of males. Yet 75 per cent of females believed that regular elections are necessary compared to 70 per cent of males, though it should be pointed out that fewer than 3 per cent disagreed with this proposition.

Although most respondents agreed that there should be equal rights for women (73 per cent), there was a large sex difference with 82 per cent of females agreeing and only 65 per cent of males who presumably felt potentially threatened by this. Similarly, 77 per cent of females disagreed compared to only 61 per cent of males with the proposition that women should stay out of politics.

Disappointingly, less than half of the sample (44 per cent) disagreed with the proposition that people from certain religious or racial groups should be kept out of politics though once again there was a dramatic sex difference with 51 per cent of females disagreeing and only 35 per cent of males. Curiously though, possibly because of their experience, females tend to be less fatalistic than males with 42 per cent of females versus 47 per cent of males agreeing that there is nothing they can do about government decisions. Yet females do believe in the compassion of government — for instance, only 44 per cent of females compared to 60 per cent of males (total 52 per cent) believe that powerful people in government do not care about the opinions of ordinary people. Thus, more females than males (32 per cent vs. 28 per cent) agreed that the government is doing its best to find out what ordinary people want, though more disagreed with this item.

As few as 61 per cent disgreed with the motion that 'Most women do not need the right to vote' though many more females than males disagreed (69 per cent vs. 52 per cent). These sex differences in opinions about political rights are highly predictable and consistent, but perhaps what is most surprising is how many respondents were undecided.

There was general agreement and very little disagreement from all respondents that people should complain to the authorities when there is something wrong (74 per cent) and that it is good for a government to be frequently criticized (79 per cent), with minimal disagreement (15 per cent and 2 per cent respectively). Half of the respondents, many more males (55 per cent) than females (43 per cent), believed that the government did not try to understand them. Similarly, just under half (46 per cent) believed that most politicians do not care about ordinary people.

The majority of the respondents disagreed with two bellicose items, namely that war is often the only way a nation can save its self-respect (51 per cent) and that if another nation does not agree with us we should fight them (61 per cent). Even more were cynical about politicians, as over two-thirds (68 per cent) disagreed with the statement that the people in power know best.

Again, females tended to be more fatalistic than males as more agreed (24 per cent vs. 21 per cent) and fewer disagreed (51 per cent vs. 55 per cent) with the idea that it will not matter whether they vote or not. However, females were much more in favour of negotiation than war as 80 per cent (compared to 74 per cent of males) agreed and only 7 per cent disagreed.

Similarly, there was general disagreement (61 per cent) that it was wrong to criticize the government, though a quarter remained undecided, presumably because they felt that it depended on specific issues. A similar number (61 per cent) disagreed with the belief that it is wrong to criticize the government because it interrupts the government's work but here there was a sex difference as fewer females (56 per cent) than males (63 per cent) tended to disagree with this.

Almost ten per cent more females (69 per cent) than males (59 per cent) disagreed with the egocentric item: 'I don't really care what happens to others, so long as I am all right', but there was no sex difference and general agreement (82 per cent) with the item 'Our nation has its faults just like every other nation'.

CONCLUDING REMARKS

This chapter has reviewed the results of a range of questions about the governing of Britain. Before attempting to draw an overall conclusion about the scepticism, cynicism, fatalism, or naivety of our respondents, four issues need to be discussed.

The first concerns differences between the responses of adults (where we have the data) and adolescents. This is not a completely fair comparison as the data were collected at different times (1983/4 and 1986/7), nevertheless some comparison is possible. To a large extent the results were similar. For instance, the rank order of how well or badly British institutions were perceived to be run was very similar as were the problems seen to be facing Britain, although our adolescent sample believed institutions were better run and problems more likely. However, compared to adults, they seemed to look more favourably on Northern Ireland and the trade unions but were more cynical about nuclear weapons and less law abiding where they believed the law to be unjust. Yet, like all adults, they were generally in favour of the monarchy and the death penalty.

Second, the issue of sex differences warrants discussion in connection with these attitudinal items. On the one hand, it may seem that the results are highly inconsistent, with females appearing both more conservative and more liberal. However, once one examines closely the contents of the items in light of the studies reviewed in chapter 2, a much clearer pattern emerges. Compared to males, females tend to be more conservative with respect to the institutions of government and law and order, more fatalistic and resigned about their ability to do much about them, and less conservative (i.e., more liberal) on issues of discrimination, feminist issues, and more enthusiastic about negotiation and egalitarianism. There were a striking number of sex differences over many of these items. Males tend to be more bellicose, more radical, and less tolerant in their views, if not their behaviour.

Third, something needs to be said about those who expressed no opinion. Somewhere between one in ten and one in three of the sample chose to express no opinion to some questions. Various reasons may be put forward: they did not understand the question; they had no opinion on the issue; or they genuinely could not decide. However, if one looks at table 3.4 it appears that the more the question tapped the experience of young people the more they answered it. Only 12 per cent did not express an opinion on whether swimming pools should admit people of all races and nationalities while 32 per cent did not express an opinion on whether the government cares about what the people think about new laws. The amount of indecision (expressed in preference for a non-committal response) may partly reflect, then, the respondents' actual political experience.

Fourth, it came as some surprise that there were so few systematic age or class differences. Over three-quarters of the sample were aged between 13 and 18 years and it may be that there are comparatively few developments in thinking about politics at this age. A vast majority of pupils are still at school and not directly involved in the political process.

Do these results show adolescents to be ignorant, sceptical, naive, or anarchic? Clearly the complexity and number of issues dealt with mean that no simple label is appropriate. It is probably true to say that the sample trust political institutions more than individual politicians and the government. Many, however, are relatively fearful about the future but few believe in war and fighting over dialogue and discussion. The respondents tended to be self-critical and critical of government but with the perhaps not unnatural feeling that at their age they could exercise little influence over political affairs.

Chapter Four

ATTITUDES CONCERNING CRIME AND LAW ENFORCEMENT

Crime and the maintenance of law and order are among the main recent concerns of the Government and the British public. A recent Gallup survey has indicated an increased pessimism among British people today who perceive the country to be getting ever more violent (Heald and Wybrow 1986). Large sections of the public seem to believe that the legal system and law enforcement agencies can no longer guarantee sufficient protection from crime and that people in the future will increasingly have to take the law into their own hands if threatened.

In addition to the growing perceptions of a violent society, substantial numbers of people say that they fear being victims of crime themselves. Fear of crime has been distinguished conceptually from judgements about possible risks from crime (Zillmann and Wakshlag 1985). The actual levels of crime in an area are not necessarily or always related to how fearful residents feel (Garofalo and Laub 1981). Heald and Wybrow report that one in three (31 per cent) of people in this country fear personal victimization either 'a great deal' or 'quite a bit'. A similar number (33 per cent) have a slight fear of crime.

When asked how safe they felt walking alone in their own neighbourhood after dark, 36 per cent of the Gallup sample said they felt 'not very' or 'not at all' safe, with the proportions rising to over one in two in the case of women and to two in three among the elderly. Fear was greater among city dwellers than among people who live in rural locations. The young (16–24s) were more likely to say they felt safe close to home.

The British Crime Survey (Hough and Mayhew 1985) included several questions about fear and crime. When asked how safe they felt when walking alone after dark in their neighbourhood, in 1983 around one in three (31 per cent) of respondents said they felt 'fairly unsafe' or 'very unsafe', a slight decrease on 1981 (34 per cent). Generally, women (48 per cent) were more likely than men (13 per cent) to feel unsafe, with very little change occurring over time. Further questions were asked about fears relating to specific types of crime. Men were less worried about being mugged (13 per cent) than about being burgled (18 per cent), while women were equally worried about both types of crime (27–8 per cent). Women generally (30 per cent), but especially young women under 30 (41 per cent), were most concerned about rape.

People were found, however, to overestimate risks of falling victim to crimes and this might have contributed to their levels of concern. Women, as noted above, were very worried about rape, but tended to hold exaggerated estimates of its likelihood which were far in excess of the statistical probability of their being victimized. Degrees of worry about burglary tended to vary depending on area of residence, suggesting that people may have some grasp of the relative likelihood of break-ins. However, personal estimates revealed that people in all areas had distorted impressions about personal risk from burglary. Overestimation of actual risks was highest in areas where burglary was relatively infrequent, with those who overestimated also expressing the greatest anxiety.

Research on the crime- and law-related attitudes of adolescents and adults have been considered within the sphere of political socialization, primarily in terms of broad sociological or personality constructs. Sociologists and political psychologists have reported relationships of age and other demographic variables to opinions or attitudes concerning governmental authority, legal and moral rights of citizens, and political cynicism (Bell 1973; Niemi 1973).

Personality psychologists have focused upon such law-related constructs as authoritarianism (Adorno et al. 1950), political liberalism (Eisenberg-Berg 1979; Mussen et al. 1977), concern with social responsibility (Berkowitz and Lutterman 1968), and the existence of a 'just world' (Lerner et al. 1970).

Adolescence may be a critical period in the development of attitudes concerning law, crime, and the judicial system. On the one hand, important changes in logical reasoning abilities and the capacity for philosophical reflection enable adolescents to adopt ideological systems of beliefs and attitudes (Adelson 1971; Inhelder and Piaget 1958) and political attitudes in general are in a formative stage (Niemi 1973). On the other hand, adolescents are likely to encounter the criminal justice system, either directly or indirectly, through peers, police, courts, or other experiences. Such encounters are likely because of the prevalence of delinquent activity among youth, conflicts between youth culture and the laws governing the use of drugs, and the assumption of legal responsibility and potential liability when the adolescent begins to drive.

Youth attitudes towards crime- and law-related matters, however, are not always simply formed. Recent research has indicated that such attitudes tend to be multidimensional. Nelson *et al.* (1982) investigated the structure of high-school students' attitudes relating to crime, law, and justice. They wanted to find out if these attitudes formed into clusters which could be clearly defined and differentiated. They gave a group of high-school students a battery of items derived from a selection of other scales (e.g., liberalism, just world, authoritarianism, and social responsibility). Respondents were required to endorse each item along a four-point agree-disagree scale. Responses were factor analysed to reveal six interpretable factors labelled retributive responses to criminals; self-attribution of social-legal responsibility; belief in effective versus ineffective law enforcement; law abidance; government by authority versus government by law; and adverse, exploitative orientation to the law.

In our survey, we probed the beliefs and attitudes of young people concerning a number of aspects of the legal and justice systems, law enforcement, and crime. Respondents were asked nine questions and presented with a further thirty-two attitude statements on each of which they indicated their agreement or disagreement. Impressions and beliefs about crime were broken down into eight categories:

1. perceptions and concern about local crime;
2. beliefs concerning crime prevention;
3. opinions concerning the police;
4. willingness to become personally involved in dealing with crime;
5. beliefs about causes of crime and criminality;
6. beliefs about justice;
7. beliefs concerning punishment for crime; and
8. opinions concerning laws against crime.

PERCEPTIONS AND CONCERN ABOUT LOCAL CRIME

The emergence in many urban and suburban areas of neighbourhood watch schemes reflects a growing concern about crime and also an awareness among people that they need to look out for each other and play an active role themselves in protecting their own locality. Crime surveys have revealed that the public do fear crime, although levels of fear do not necessarily coincide with the actual occurrence of crime. Anxieties vary also with the type of crime and the circumstances under which personal victimization might occur. But what about young people — what do they think about the chances of falling prey to criminal elements? Do the youth of today worry about crime?

Under the heading of perceptions and concern about local crime, we asked our youth sample six questions about the occurrence of crime in their own neighbourhood and put to them four more items which dealt with their opinions and concerns relating to crime where they lived.

In a general sense around half (51 per cent) said that they worried at least sometimes that either they themselves or someone they lived with might be the victim of crime. There was no marked tendency for females (53 per cent) to be worried more often than males (51 per cent). On a more clearly distinguished local level, however, a strong sex difference emerged. A majority (57 per cent) said they felt safe walking alone after dark in their own neighbourhood, but this feeling was much more commonplace among males (74 per cent) than among females (37 per cent). In general, most respondents did not perceive neighbourhood burglary (60 per cent) or neighbourhood muggings (71 per cent) to be very common. Local vandalism, however, was seen to be more commonplace. Forty-eight per cent felt that it was fairly or very common for deliberate damage to be done to local properties; almost 41 per cent did not think it was very common.

Among young people in general somewhat more (37 per cent) felt there was only a remote chance of one of their family or close friends being the victim of an assault during the next year than those who held a more pessimistic point of view (23 per cent). Males (55 per cent) were more optimistic about this than were females (38 per cent).

Despite the fact that the perceived likelihood of victimization for others was not widespread, there was some evidence of concern about local dangers. The proportion of young people who wanted more money spent on local police patrols (39 per cent) exceeded those who did not (27 per cent), while more (35 per cent) were worried about being burgled than who were not (23 per cent). A majority (57 per cent) also agreed that local parks are not safe places to let children play, compared to 21 per cent who were not concerned about this.

There were two striking sex differences. First of all, females (62 per cent) were more often concerned than males (50 per cent) about letting children play in local parks. Second, males (28 per cent) were more likely than females (19 per cent) to say that they were *not* worried about being burgled.

BELIEFS CONCERNING CRIME PREVENTION

There may be many reasons for rising crime. In addition to various social, environmental, and psychological reasons, there is the extent to which measures of crime prevention and crime avoidance, on the part of both law enforcement agencies and the public, deter or otherwise restrict the opportunities of criminal elements.

We gave our sample three statements about crime prevention with which to agree or disagree. First, 'it is the duty of each person to help prevent crime and maintain law and order'. Second, 'stricter policing is the best way to prevent crime'. And third, 'the man who provides temptation by leaving valuable property unprotected is about as much to blame for its theft as the one who steals it'.

Most adolescents (61 per cent) held the opinion that stricter policing was the best way to prevent crime. Females (67 per cent) believed this more than males (57 per cent). There was a feeling also that ordinary people could play an important part (63 per cent) in the prevention of crime and maintenance of law and order. Finally, carelessness on the part of individuals in looking after personal belongings was thought to be in no small way to blame for criminal theft (55 per cent). Males (58 per cent) were marginally more likely than females (50 per cent) to believe this.

OPINIONS CONCERNING THE POLICE

To what extent have young people had personal dealings with the police and what impressions do they have? Around one in three (34 per cent) said they had either reported a crime to the police or gone to them for help or advice during the previous two years. Among these individuals more (52 per cent) had found the police helpful than unhelpful (34 per cent). Opinions hardly differed between males and females, though the latter were slightly more likely to have had personal dealings with the police.

More than four out of ten (44 per cent) claimed they had been questioned by the police about a crime during the previous two years. Here there was a marked sex difference, with many more males (58 per cent) than females (31 per cent) having had this sort of contact with the police. Among those who had helped the police with their enquiries, more had found the police to be impolite (47 per cent) than polite (39 per cent). Males (53 per cent) were more likely to complain about police manners than were females (35 per cent).

Table 4.1 Opinions concerning the police

	All %	Male %	Female %
During the past two years have you ever reported a crime or accident to the police or gone to them for help or advice?			
Yes	34	36	30
No	66	64	70
Among yesses: on those occasions, how helpful did you find the police in the way they dealt with you?			
Generally very helpful	16	15	17
Generally fairly helpful	37	37	38
Generally fairly unhelpful	20	20	19
Generally very unhelpful	15	16	14
Sometimes helpful/sometimes unhelpful	12	12	12
During the past two years have you ever been stopped or asked questions by the police about an offence which they thought had been committed?			
Yes	44	58	31
No	56	42	69
Among yesses: on those occasions, were the police polite or impolite when they approached you?			
Generally very polite	12	7	19
Generally fairly polite	28	26	35
Generally fairly impolite	24	23	25
Generally very impolite	23	30	10
Sometimes polite/sometimes impolite	13	14	12

WILLINGNESS TO BECOME PERSONALLY INVOLVED IN DEALING WITH CRIME

Earlier opinions about the personal responsibilities of the public in preventing crime might lead one to expect that young people would be likely to exhibit further indications of willingness to fight crime. To find out if this was so, we probed our youth sample further about their attitudes towards personal crime-fighting or prevention.

Table 4.2 Willingness to become personally involved in dealing with crime

	All %	*Male* %	*Female* %
If I witness a crime, I keep my mouth shut because I don't want to become involved			
Agree	37	45	28
Neither	23	20	26
Disagree	40	35	46
I would volunteer to testify in a trial, if I had witnessed a crime or an accident			
Agree	58	52	67
Neither	24	24	21
Disagree	18	24	12
If I saw someone shop-lifting, I would report it to the authorities			
Agree	44	44	51
Neither	28	28	28
Disagree	28	28	21
If I were asked to serve on a jury, I would try to get out of it			
Agree	31	33	30
Neither	27	29	25
Disagree	42	38	45
I feel badly when I have witnessed a minor crime and failed to report it			
Agree	41	40	44
Neither	35	31	39
Disagree	24	29	17
It is no use worrying about crimes and legal affairs; I can't do anything about them anyway			
Agree	36	31	40
Neither	31	36	27
Disagree	33	33	33

It is apparent that young people are more willing to join in the fight against crime in some ways than in others. Most (58 per cent) would volunteer to testify in a trial as witnesses; females (67 per cent) more especially than males (52 per cent). More, though not a majority (44 per cent), would report someone they saw shop-lifting than would not (28 per cent). The difference between the sexes is interesting here. A majority of females (51 per cent) would report a witnessed shop theft, while males (45 per cent) would be more likely not to.

The largest proportion (41 per cent) said they would feel badly if they witnessed a minor crime and failed to report it and disagreed that they would keep out of it, if they witnessed a crime. On the last item, however, females (46 per cent) were more likely to want to do the right thing than were males (35 per cent).

BELIEFS ABOUT CAUSES OF CRIME AND CRIMINALITY

Among young people there is clearly some feeling that the efficiency of law enforcement and personal crime prevention measures contribute to some extent to current levels of crime. But, in a broader social or psychological sense, are criminals a special breed who originate from a certain kind of background?

We asked our adolescent sample whether they agreed or disagreed with each of these statements. First, 'crime is more often the fault of our society than the fault of the criminal'. Second, 'most criminals will never be able to live right no matter how much we do for them'. Third, 'crime is caused by people without morals or standards'.

Although not held by an overwhelming majority, the weight of opinion among young people interviewed in this survey was that crime is caused by people without morals or standards. Agreement with this (37 per cent) was more common than disagreement (28 per cent). Even more prevalent (44 per cent) was the belief that criminals cannot be 'made good', with 29 per cent disagreeing. But the criminal is not himself or herself totally to blame. In the view of nearly half (48 per cent) the respondents, crime is more often the fault of society than of the criminal. Only 24 per cent disagreed with this statement. There were no sex, age, or class differences for any of these opinions.

BELIEFS ABOUT JUSTICE

Table 4.3 Beliefs about justice

	All %	Male %	Female %
1. Even if a man is guilty, the police should make sure he gets all his rights			
Agree	72	73	69
Neither	16	15	19
Disagree	12	12	12
2. Crime doesn't pay			
Agree	66	61	75
Neither	19	19	17
Disagree	15	20	8
3. I get pretty discouraged with the law when a smart lawyer gets a criminal free			
Agree	60	60	60
Neither	27	28	26
Disagree	13	12	14
4. Judges and courts do not give fair and equal treatment to everyone in this country			
Agree	58	58	57
Neither	28	24	31
Disagree	14	18	12
5. It is rare for an innocent man to be wrongly sent to jail			
Agree	46	45	47
Neither	27	28	26
Disagree	27	27	27
6. It is a common occurrence for a guilty person to get off free in British courts			
Agree	41	46	39
Neither	34	30	36
Disagree	25	24	25
7. Law-breakers are almost always caught and punished			
Agree	35	34	36
Neither	25	21	30
Disagree	40	45	34
8. It doesn't do any good to co-operate with the police because criminals usually aren't punished for their crimes			
Agree	31	33	29
Neither	31	30	32
Disagree	38	37	39
9. It is often impossible for a person to receive a fair trial in the United Kingdom			
Agree	28	30	24
Neither	31	28	35
Disagree	41	42	41

Does the system of law and justice deal effectively with law-breakers? Does crime pay? Are criminals or those accused of crime given a fair deal? Having investigated what young people have to say about crime, we turned finally to examine their views about the legal and justice systems. On the whole, young people felt that the world is a place where criminal elements are not always dealt with effectively. At the same time, however, there were some disparate opinions and differences of opinion among respondents.

Among the opinions held most commonly were that even the guilty have their rights (72 per cent), crime doesn't pay (66 per cent), and discouragement with the law when a smart lawyer gets a criminal free (60 per cent). Males (83 per cent) were keener to see a guilty man getting his rights than were females (69 per cent), while females (75 per cent) were more often of the view that crime doesn't pay than were males (61 per cent).

There was not total belief in the system of justice. Certainly, more (46 per cent) believed that it is rare for the innocent to go to jail than who did not (27 per cent), and fewer (28 per cent) agreed that it is impossible for a person in this country to receive a fair trial than those who disagreed (41 per cent). But most young people (58 per cent) felt that the courts do not treat everyone fairly and equally more agreed (41 per cent) than disagreed (25 per cent) that it is common for the guilty to go free, also more disagreed (40 per cent) than agreed (35 per cent) that law-breakers are almost always caught and punished. Finally, there were mixed opinions about how useful it is to co-operate with the police since criminals usually aren't effectively punished anyway.

BELIEFS CONCERNING PUNISHMENT FOR CRIME

The lack of faith in the justice system to deal effectively with criminals and to allocate punishments to fit the severity of crimes was widely evident. It further emerged that young people are largely in favour of strict punishments for serious crimes. Most (66 per cent) endorsed capital punishment for murderers; 18 per cent were against this. Most (62 per cent) were also in favour of severe punishments (e.g. public whipping) for rapists and child molesters, while just 16 per cent were opposed. Finally, a majority (61 per cent) supported strict enforcement of all existing laws. Females were more in favour than were males both of capital punishment for murderers (70 per cent versus 65 per cent) and of strict law enforcement generally (65 per cent versus 57 per cent).

OPINIONS CONCERNING LAWS AGAINST CRIME

Our youth sample were not simply in favour of strict law enforcement, most (69 per cent) also felt that there should be tougher laws against crime in this country. Nine per cent were against tougher laws. According to nearly two out of three (63 per cent), everybody should take part in the development and enforcement of laws for the good of local communities and the country as a whole, while 11 per cent were not keen on this. A weight of opinion (46 per cent) indicated that these young people felt that laws were not enough; 36 per cent were unsure and 18 per cent disagreed. According to 46 per cent, the country also needed strong, courageous, and trustworthy leaders in whom people could put their faith, while 21 per cent disagreed and 33 per cent were undecided.

CONCLUDING REMARKS

An interesting picture of young people's opinions concerning crime, law enforcement, and justice emerged from this survey which indicated a widespread awareness of the problems of crime and a tendency to be in favour of stricter law enforcement and penalties for those who break the law. A majority of our respondents said they worried about the possibility of being involved (as victims) in crime. They were concerned for their own safety and for that of relatives and close friends. Although most did not feel that they were likely to be victims of crime in the foreseeable future, they were nevertheless wary of the dangers that exist in society today. A substantial minority were concerned in particular about crime close to home. In general, females were more likely than males to be anxious about personal safety; this finding is consistent with the results of other surveys (Hough and Mayhew 1985).

Perhaps as a consequence of perceived dangers from crime, some need was felt for more protection in the local environment from police. A wider view was that stricter policing was the best way to prevent crime. However, ordinary people were believed to carry some of this responsibility too and to be able to play an important part in the fight against crime. Personal negligence on the part of individuals in how they take care of property and belongings was seen as a contributory factor in the encouragement of crime.

Many of our respondents reported that they had had contact with the police, who were perceived to be helpful more often than not though perhaps not always as polite as they might be. Despite this, young people seem to be willing personally to join in the fight against crime — but in some ways more than in others. Many said they would not feel good about failing to report a crime they had witnessed. This would not, apparently, prevent them from not getting involved in some cases. Although most said they would be prepared to volunteer as witnesses at a trial, they would be much less likely to report someone they saw shop-lifting.

In addition to probing their opinions connected with personal involvement with crime and crime-prevention, we also tried to find out young people's views about the causes of crime and efficiency of the legal and justice system in a much broader sense. By and large, our respondents felt that crime is caused by people without morals or standards. The criminal character was thought to be in part inherited and in part shaped by the social environment. Thus, respondents felt that criminals cannot be cured, but are not totally to blame for their anti-social tendencies.

Our sample of young people did not seem to have total faith in the criminal justice system, which was seen to have both merits and faults. This was manifested in a number of conflicting beliefs about standards of justice in this country. For instance, most felt that crime doesn't pay, while at the same time there was widespread disillusionment that smart lawyers can and do get criminals off the hook. Most respondents felt that it is rare for the innocent to go to jail and that fair trials in this country are the rule. But there was a common belief that not everyone is treated fairly in the courts. Many respondents held the opinion that the guilty often go free, but law-breakers are usually caught and punished in the end.

Our young people were in favour of strict penalties for serious crimes. Most supported capital punishment for major offenders such as murderers, rapists, and child molesters. Many felt that in general the laws of the land are not tough enough. The country needed strong leaders who also had the courage to introduce a tough system of legal penalties to punish offenders. This would not be successfully implemented, however, without the support of the population.

Chapter Five

BRITAIN AND EUROPE

The European Community (EEC) came into being with the Treaty of Rome which was signed by France, West Germany, Italy, The Netherlands, Luxembourg, and Belgium in March 1957. Over fifteen years later, in 1973, Ireland, Denmark, and Great Britain joined the community. This event heralded a new era in the relationship between Britain and Europe. Throughout the past four centuries Britain had been at war with one or other European state including France, Germany, Holland, Italy, and Spain. Now, over forty years after the ending of the Second World War, Britain, in some sense, has become part of Europe.

There has always been in Britain a certain amount of antipathy towards Europe, and indeed towards ever considering Britain as part of Europe. Whereas many statesmen like Churchill and Bevin have been pro-Europeans, the average citizen has been doubtful. As early as 1888 Gladstone argued 'We are part of the Community of Europe, and we must do our duty as such'. Yet the famous *Times* headline 'Fog in Channel, Europe isolated' probably captures more of the spirit of British attitudes to Europe. Barzini has put this more eloquently: 'In a way Britain still sees itself as the sceptred isle cut from the Continent by divine will. If God had wanted to tie it to the rest of Europe, He would evidently have dug a tunnel' (Barzini 1983: 59).

There are many reasons why we were interested in young people's attitudes to Europe. First, nearly all the studies on people's attitude to the EEC have been done on adults (over 18) and the views of young people (pre-voters) have been largely ignored. Second, more than in any other generation, young people have been to the continent — not only on day-trips to France but on holidays in Portugal and Spain as well as visits to the Low Countries. Whereas their parents found themselves in Europe often only to fight a war, young Britons have visited the continent and met Europeans on a quite different basis. Third, many young people have known no other Britain than one that is part of the EEC. Though they may not be particularly conscious of EEC affairs, or indeed know who their Euro-MP is, issues concerning EEC affairs are very frequently discussed.

. As has been noted, the relatively few studies on British attitudes to Europe have been done almost exclusively on adults. These studies fall into two groups. Since 1974 the EEC has collected and published public opinion throughout the community by asking the same accurately translated questions in the different member countries at the same time. These results are useful because they provide comparisons between public opinion of member countries at any *one point* in time; they provide longitudinal data *over time*, and they are broken down by age, sex, class, etc., so demonstrating differences within countries. The second sort of study, looking at British attitudes to the EEC, has been smaller in scale in terms of the number of respondents, but has tended to focus on wider issues and undertake more sophisticated statistical analyses.

THE EURO-BAROMETRE

The Euro-Barometre reports have concerned a very wide range of issues, such as the mood of Europeans, their political values and attitudes as well as their attitudes to Europe. However, on a number of issues tested over time (since 1974) attitudes in Britain appear to be somewhat different from those of the other major European countries: for instance, in answer to the question 'In general are you for or against efforts being made to unify Western Europe? If for, are you very much for, or only to some extent? If against, are you only to some extent against, or very much against?' Although there are some interesting fluctuations over time, the trend is pretty clear. This can be seen in the 1979 results which looked at how much support there was for European integration: Italy (66 per cent); West Germany (43 per cent); France (35 per cent); and Britain (28 per cent). Another question about EEC membership yielded much the same pattern of results. The question was 'Generally speaking, do you think that [your country's] membership of the EEC is a good thing, a bad thing, or neither good nor bad?' In 1985, 72 per cent of Italians, 68 per cent of the French, and 54 per cent of Germans thought that it was a good thing compared to only 37 per cent of the British. The average for the ten EEC countries was 57 per cent.

The majority of the British also believe that their country has not benefited from membership of the community. Predictably, the British are less willing to make personal sacrifices (increased taxes) to help out another EEC country. Asked the question 'Do you ever think of yourself as a citizen of Europe? Often, sometimes or never?', 74 per cent of the British, 45 per cent of Italians, 40 per cent of the French, and 26 per cent of Germans said never. Hewstone has argued that:

> The British are *not* anti-European, but they are *not* pro-Community; their responses to so many of the above questions show how concerned they still are with matters of national sovereignty, and how reluctant they are to give any real, lasting commitment to the Community. (Hewstone 1986: 38)

SPECIFIC STUDIES

The Euro-Barometre provides interesting data but is limited to a large sample of respondents answering a few questions. In smaller-scale studies researchers have attempted to look at such things as the *structure* of British attitudes to Europe. Wober interviewed 813 people about their attitudes to Europe. This representative sample was given sixteen questions in all, relating to a wide variety of issues. As predicted, there was an underlying structure to these questions which fell into three groups — those concerned with economic, political, and cultural matters. Wober then looked at the way various personal characteristics related to those three attitudinal clusters about the EEC.

> More particularly, men and women do not differ in respect of cultural or political attitudes concerning Europe, but women appear to have more support for economic integration than men do. Age does not relate to economic attitudes, but older people are better disposed on political matters though less pro-European on cultural topics than are younger adults. People of higher socio-economic status are clearly better disposed towards Europe than are lower status adults — on cultural matters; but the relationship is reversed as regards support for political integration; and no relation exists between class and attitudes in the economic sphere, regarding Europe.

TV viewing overall (a measure which usually correlates with amount of news and current affairs viewing) relates in opposite ways to cultural and economic attitudes to Europe. Heavier viewers (similarly people of lower social class, and older people) tend to be less in favour of the 'cultural perspective' on Europe than are light viewers; the lightest viewers are not well disposed on economic matters to Europe, though they are in favour of integration in cultural matters. Heavy radio listening (which again usually correlates with amount of news listening) associates with more positive attitudes to Europe on all three dimensions, though most markedly in the case of the economic items. Knowledge and voting are related to approval of cultural aspects of integration with Europe, but not to economic or political matters. (Wober 1981: 186–7)

In a later study, Wober (1986) set out to discover whether attitudes to Europe are distinguishable from attitudes to the EEC. He found that, although attitudes towards the EEC do correlate with aspects of attitudes towards integration between Britain and Europe, the two show substantially different ways of relating to criteria such as interest in the election campaign on television, knowledge of the member countries, and claims of having voted.

Perhaps the most thorough study concerning understanding of attitudes to the EEC was done by Hewstone (1986). The study concentrated on the attitudes of university students from Britain, France, Germany, and Italy. On many of the measures that he looked at he found the British significantly different from and less pro-European than respondents in the other three countries. He also found overall the students, who were of course well educated and intelligent, a consistent pattern of low interest and poor knowledge, indicating that in the minds of young people the EEC was of little relevance. In order to try and predict people's overall attitudes to the EEC, Hewstone developed path models which took into consideration such factors as people's liking of the EEC, their national image, the amount of contact they had with other Europeans, their support, etc. He found, as have so many others, that more than other groups the British lacked support for the community. Various reasons are put forward to account for this:

history — different experience of war as well as the fact that relative decline in Britain has coincided with community membership is one possible explanation for late membership and negative attitudes;

financial problems — the British feel the budget and the agricultural policy are poor and inequitable in the sense that they contribute more than they receive;

politicians — past politicians and more particularly Margaret Thatcher have not been seen to be pro-European and have done little to foster a sense of European solidarity;

relations with France — consistent and long-standing distrust of the French (which is probably mutual) has meant that conflictual relations have acted as a barrier to the development of identitive support;

role of the press — although the British press appears to cover EEC affairs fairly extensively, it appears to be less favourable than in other countries and fuels the fires of protectionism and nationalism;

scapegoat — the EEC is often an alibi for prevailing discontents and for politicians when difficult decisions have to be made or things are going badly.

In our survey of young people's attitudes to, and knowledge of, the EEC we were interested in a number of different issues. These were:

how successful/unsuccessful the EEC has been;
the gains and losses of Britain by joining the EEC;
Britain's relationship with the EEC;
which countries benefit most and least from membership;
which European countries are, and are not, EEC members;
economic attitudes to the EEC;
cultural attitudes to the EEC;
political attitudes to the EEC.

HOW SUCCESSFUL AND UNSUCCESSFUL HAS THE EEC BEEN?

We gave respondents four statements concerning various features of EEC policy. First, 'the EEC has made reasonably priced food available for consumers'; second, 'the EEC has increased efficiency of industries'; third, 'the EEC has made a lot of movement possible for people to work in each others' countries'; and fourth, 'the EEC has spoken with a single voice in dealing with other world powers and problems'. Overall, more agreed (46 per cent) than disagreed (19 per cent) that the EEC had made reasonably priced food available though over a third (35 per cent) expressed no opinion. Even more, nearly 50 per cent, had no opinion as to whether the EEC increased the efficiency of industries or not, though about a third agreed (33 per cent) and a fifth (19 per cent) disagreed.

Nearly half (46 per cent) of the respondents felt the EEC made more movement between countries possible so that citizens could work in more countries. Again, however, a large number (44 per cent) did not express an opinion, and a minority (10 per cent) disagreed. Almost as many agreed (26 per cent) as disagreed (24 per cent) with the final assertion that the EEC has spoken with a single voice with exactly half (50 per cent) of the sample expressing no opinion. There were no class or age differences to these questions but the last one did show a sex difference. Males (28 per cent) agreed more strongly than females (22 per cent) that the EEC spoke with a single voice.

These results show a mixture of either ignorance or apathy, given the very large number of respondents unable to agree or disagree. However, though the majority was low in the last question, overall the respondents tended to agree with the proposition that the EEC had been relatively successful with respect to food prices, industrial efficiency, movement for work, and giving a collective viewpoint on world affairs.

THE GAINS AND LOSSES OF BRITAIN BY JOINING THE EEC

A central issue, no doubt, for each member country is whether membership of the EEC involves net gains or losses. We asked our respondents four questions concerning the net gains of British membership. Did they agree or disagree that (1) 'Britain pays much more into the EEC budget than we get out of it'; (2) 'Britain has benefited from the EEC'; (3) 'Britain has gained from the EEC's Community Regional Fund'; (4) 'Britain has become less competitive as a result of belonging to the EEC'?

A majority of 60 per cent agreed that Britain pays more into the budget than gets out of it. Only 4 per cent disagreed, but a third (36 per cent) expressed no opinion. More males (61 per cent) than females (56 per cent) agreed with this proposition. But when asked the question more generally about overall benefits of joining the EEC, 30 per cent agreed and 23 per cent disagreed, with nearly half (47 per cent) expressing no opinion. Well over half, in fact 60 per cent, neither agreed nor disagreed with the statement that Britain had gained from the EEC's Community Regional Fund presumably because they did not know anything about it. But more agreed (26 per cent) than disagreed (14 per cent) with the proposition. The same pattern of results emerged in the last question where half (50 per cent) expressed no opinion but nearly a third (32 per cent) agreed, and 18 per cent disagreed that Britain had become less competitive as a result of belonging to the EEC. In this sense, the EEC may be seen by some as an excuse for Britain's relative economic decline.

BRITAIN'S RELATIONSHIP WITH THE EEC

We also asked four questions about how Britain gets on with the EEC as a whole. Did they agree or disagree that (1) 'I have a growing feeling of solidarity between myself and citizens of other EEC countries'; (2) 'the EEC interferes unjustifiably with the national government of the UK'; (3) 'the EEC can be trusted to look after the interest of the UK'; (4) 'the EEC have mishandled economic affairs'? The responses on all four questions were remarkably similar. About a quarter agreed (23–8 per cent) with both the two positive statements — a feeling of solidarity with other EEC citizens (25 per cent) and the EEC can be trusted to look after British interests — but also with the negative statements — that the EEC interferes unjustifiably (28 per cent) and has mishandled economic affairs (25 per cent). Again, for each question about a half (47–59 per cent) neither agreed nor disagreed and between a fifth and a third (19–30 per cent) disagreed. They disagreed most (30 per cent) that the EEC can be trusted to look after the interests of the UK.

There was, however, a consistent sex difference for each question; males always agreed more than females, particularly with respect to the two negative items — the EEC interferes unjustifiably and it has mishandled the economy — where the gulf was fairly large. Overall, it seemed that males were more happy to express an opinion than females, though a large number still neither agreed nor disagreed.

WHICH COUNTRIES BENEFIT MOST AND
LEAST FROM MEMBERSHIP

We were particularly interested in our respondents' perceptions of equity with respect to EEC contributions and benefits. Hence we asked which of the then nine member countries benefited and contributed most and least. The results are particularly interesting. France was seen by 41 per cent to benefit most and Eire by only 17 per cent to benefit most. Less than a fifth thought Britain benefited most (19 per cent). But, whereas the smallest number (21 per cent) thought France benefited least, a not dissimilar number — exactly 25 per cent — thought Britain benefited least. Belgium, Denmark, Eire, and Holland were the four relatively small countries thought by over a third of the respondents to benefit least.

Perhaps it is the inputs (contributions) side of the equation, rather than the outputs (benefits), that reveal most passion and bigotry. Predictably, nearly half of the respondents saw Britain as contributing the most, though over a third (35 per cent) correctly nominated Germany as the country that contributed the most. Nearly a third thought Luxembourg contributed least, followed by Eire. Only 13 per cent of the sample thought Britain contributed the least.

Table 5.1 Britain and Europe

Among the following members countries, which do you think benefits most, and least, from being in the EEC; and which do you think contributes most, and which contributes least?

	Country that benefits most %	Country that benefits least %	Country that contributes most %	Country that contributes least %
Belgium	34	41	13	12
Denmark	19	36	27	18
Eire	17	39	23	21
France	41	21	23	15
Germany	28	28	34	10
Holland	22	39	24	15
Italy	29	29	24	18
Luxembourg	18	31	20	31
United Kingdom	13	25	49	13

If we look at table 5.1 row by row, we can see our respondents' intuitive equity judgements for each country. If we contrast the five smaller countries — Belgium, Denmark, Eire, Holland, and Luxembourg — with the four bigger countries — France, Germany, Italy, and Britain — an interesting pattern emerges. With the exception of Belgium, more respondents think the smaller countries contribute more than they receive in benefits. Of the bigger countries France and Italy are seen to be net beneficiaries and Germany and Britain net contributors to the EEC. As one may expect, it is Britain that shows one of the most polarized responses. Like adults, our adolescent respondents tended to feel that Britain (and to a lesser extent Germany) got a bad deal out of EEC membership while France was a net beneficiary.

Of course these figures can be compared with actual statistics on contributions and benefits, though these are immensely complex even if simple monetary figures alone are considered. However, it is probably safe to say that our sample are fairly inaccurate in their estimations and that Britain is not as inequitably benefited as they believe.

WHICH EUROPEAN COUNTRIES ARE, AND ARE NOT, EEC MEMBERS

Earlier on in the questionnaire, we tried to establish our respondents' basic knowledge about actually who were EEC members. At the time of the survey Spain and Portugal were negotiating or had recently joined. Overall, our respondents did fairly well, the majority getting the members correct in the following order: Britain (82 per cent), France (77 per cent), Germany (74 per cent), Belgium (72 per cent), Italy (67 per cent), Denmark (67 per cent), Luxembourg (67 per cent). We did have a few trick questions — for instance, we left out Holland and put Ireland and Eire, and there was some difference between the latter, too — 48 per cent said Ireland was a member and 55 per cent Eire. Between one in five (Finland 20 per cent) and one in three (Sweden 31 per cent) thought the Scandinavian countries were part of the EEC while one in three thought Switzerland had EEC membership and even one in five (20 per cent) thought Yugoslavia was a member.

Between one in five and one in three of the respondents did not know the answer. The countries that showed the lowest 'Don't know' answer were respectively: Britain (13 per cent), Germany (19 per cent), France (19 per cent), Belgium (22 per cent), Denmark (22 per cent),

Italy (23 per cent), Luxembourg (24 per cent) — almost the exact same order as those who correctly identified those countries as members. By contrast, those countries that received the highest 'Don't know' score were Monaco (40 per cent), Finland (37 per cent), Norway (35 per cent), Austria (34 per cent), and Yugoslavia (34 per cent). Overall, the respondents appeared to have a moderately good knowledge of who were EEC members and who were not, though roughly equal numbers thought some non-EEC members like Sweden and Switzerland to be members, not members, or did not know.

Table 5.2 Britain and Europe

Which of these countries is a member of the EEC and which is not a member?

	Is %	*Is not* %	*Don't know* %
France	77	5	19
Ireland	48	28	24
Portugal	29	39	32
United Kingdom	82	5	13
Iceland	15	56	30
Austria	23	42	34
Spain	44	31	26
Monaco	9	51	40
Belgium	72	7	22
Luxembourg	67	10	24
Yugoslavia	20	46	34
Denmark	67	12	22
Italy	67	10	23
Sweden	31	38	31
Germany	74	7	19
Norway	25	39	35
Greece	31	37	31
Switzerland	32	37	31
Eire	55	6	29
Finland	20	43	37

ECONOMIC ATTITUDES TO THE EEC

Following Wober (1981), we asked six questions concerning economic aspects of EEC policy. Four of the six questions concerned either joining up with 'opposite numbers' in Europe or 'getting closer to them'. The first question concerned whether the Europeans should attempt to be economically self-sufficient with respect to food production and not to have to rely on imports from the Third World. Nearly two-thirds (65 per cent) of our respondents agreed with this and more than one in five (22 per cent) disagreed, possibly because the question was ambiguous in that the question suggests that Europe should not export food to the needy Third World

Just over half the respondents (and more males than females) believed that because European industries were more efficient than British industries their management procedures should be followed. Approximately equal numbers either disagreed or expressed no opinion. But less than half the respondents believed British unions should follow the example of the European unions who had, supposedly, got a better deal for their members. There was a sex difference on this item with more males (52 per cent) agreeing and fewer disagreeing than females (45 per cent).

Table 5.3 Economic attitudes

	Agree %	Neither %	Disagree %
With famines and population explosions coming in Africa and Asia we should concentrate on farming our own food in Europe	65	13	22
European industries have become a lot more efficient than ours and we should get closer to their ways of management	56	22	24
Unions in Europe have got a much better deal for their members than ours have done and British unions should get closer to them and their ways	49	28	23
Nationalized industries in this country should join up with their opposite numbers in Europe to try and make production cheaper	61	15	24
Large private industries in this country should join up with their opposite numbers in Europe to try and make production cheaper	56	15	29
European countries should work out a way for us all eventually to have the same money, whether it is called pounds, francs, marks, or whatever	57	12	31

There was general agreement (61 per cent) that British and European nationalized industries should join up to make production cheaper. Females agreed more than males (65 per cent vs. 56 per cent) on this item.

Almost identical numbers agreed and disagreed with the final two items in this section. Just over half agreed (56 per cent) and a third disagreed (29 per cent) with the idea that large private industries should co-operate more to make production cheaper. Also, surprisingly perhaps given the ethnocentricism and distrust of so many British respondents, nearly 60 per cent agreed on the need for a single monetary unit whatever it was called.

By and large, the majority of our respondents have positive attitudes to closer economic union with Europe, no doubt because, as the questions were framed, they perceive a certain amount of economic benefit from the act.

CULTURAL ATTITUDES TO THE EEC

Of all the questions that we asked about Britain and the EEC in our survey, perhaps those which showed fewest non-committal ('neither') answers, and those which showed consistent sex (but not class or age) differences, were those on 'cultural' attitudes to the EEC.

About two in three respondents (64 per cent), and more males than females (68 per cent vs. 60 per cent) agreed that there ought to be a European super-football league. Even more agreed (73 per cent) with the statement that the British should receive more European TV programmes, though significantly more females agreed than males. This sex difference was even more noticeable in the case of the learning of foreign languages where 82 per cent of females agreed compared to only 66 per cent of males. This no doubt reflects female interest in languages and is encouraging given the British resolute monoglottism. Again, over two in three (68 per cent) were in favour of metric units throughout the EEC with more females (72 per cent) than males (66 per cent) being in favour. This is a slightly higher number than were in favour of a common currency. It is also probable that the number is much higher than one may expect from adults who are, in all probability, far less acquainted with the metric system.

Surprisingly, only 56 per cent wished to see more foreign food and wine in the shops, though there was a large sex difference with females (56 per cent) being more gastronomically adventurous than males (31 per cent). Just under one in three of the total sample disagreed with this item.

However, whereas our sample seemed fairly eager to adopt a similar monetary and measurement unit, they were against (62 per cent) changing over to driving on the other side of the road. Despite the fact that probably the vast majority of the respondents were not car drivers, this issue certainly provoked a status quo response.

Table 5.4 Cultural attitudes

	Agree %	Neither %	Disagree %
In a few years there ought to be a European super-football league	64	17	19
It's a good thing for British viewers that our TV has European song contests, operas, and other musical programmes shown in Europe	73	9	18
Britons should learn one or more of the important European languages	73	8	19
We should settle on units like metres, grams, and litres as soon as possible so that people from other European countries can understand each others' measures	68	12	20
British shops should offer a lot more French, German, and Italian food and wines	56	13	31
Within the next few years we in Britain should change over to driving on the right-hand side of the road to be in line with most other countries	26	12	62

POLITICAL ATTITUDES TO THE EEC

Finally, we were interested in various political perceptions of the EEC. What is noticeable about table 5.5 is that, with the exception of the first question, more of the subjects disagreed with the items than agreed with them. Under half (45 per cent) believed European armies should get even closer together to rival the superpowers. Fewer females (42 per cent) than males (48 per cent) agreed with this item, possibly because of the bellicose nature of this question. However, over 50 per cent or more disagreed with the other three questions concerning a stronger European parliament, Britain being 'ruled' by a European parliament to stop the 'troubles' in Northern Ireland, and the playing of the European national anthem alongside that of the British national anthem. Males (41 per cent) more than females (27 per cent) thought that the European parliament should be made stronger. Also more males (35 per cent) compared to females (27 per cent) believed that the national and European anthems should be played together. Certainly, our respondents did not appear to be very eager for a closer political union with the EEC and the strengthening of a pan-European state.

Table 5.5 Political attitudes

	Agree %	Neither %	Disagree %
European armies should get together so that we could become a third force as strong as those of America and Communist countries	45	19	36
The European Parliament should be made stronger and have a European Prime Minister and Government, while Westminster, Edinburgh, and Cardiff should become places with more regional assemblies	34	13	53
The end of the fighting in Northern Ireland is most likely to happen if England, Wales, Scotland, Northern Ireland, and Eire are all ruled by a European Parliament	28	20	52
Whenever the national anthem is played, the European anthem should be played as well	31	19	50

CONCLUDING REMARKS

What do young Britons think about the EEC? What do they know about the Community? Do they think Britain is equitably or inequitably dealt with by membership of the EEC? Are they broadly in favour of a closer union, the status quo, or leaving the Common Market?

Though we only had a limited number of questions to use to investigate the above issues, the results go some way to answering the question. Most of our sample had a fair idea which countries were, and which were not, members of the Community. But their attitudes to the EEC do seem equivocal. By and large, the respondents felt that the EEC had been successful, especially in economic terms, and were in favour of closer economic and cultural ties. Yet there was the general perception that Britain gained less and lost more by joining the EEC. There was also considerable hesitancy about losing sovereignty to a European parliament.

Three issues warrant some discussion. The first concerns how different the attitudes of our adolescent sample were from those of British adults. Comparing the economic, cultural, and political attitudes of a large adult sample (Wober 1986) with those of our study there are striking similarities. For instance, in both samples the greatest agreement was with the statement 'The British should learn one or more of the important European languages', while the statement that both adults *and* adolescents disagreed with most was 'The end of the fighting in Northern Ireland is most likely to happen if England, Wales, Scotland, Northern Ireland, and Eire are all ruled by a European Parliament'. Similarly, results from the British samples published in the Euro-Barometre suggest that there is a considerable amount of agreement in the responses of adults and adolescents. If this is the case, it suggests that attitudes to the EEC are formed very early and remain largely unchanged, monitored perhaps by the ubiquitous media.

Second, we found evidence of sex differences but fewer age and class differences than one may expect by chance. Where there were sex differences, a fairly consistent pattern emerged. Females tended to be less distrustful of the EEC, less chauvinistic and patriotic, and more in favour of closer union. These results are broadly in line with other studies on sex differences in socio-political attitudes (see chapters 2 and 3). Perhaps it is most surprising that there were so few age differences, indicating that there was no systematic difference between the responses of our youngest group (aged 10–14 years) and our eldest group (aged 17 +). Again, this suggests that attitudes to the EEC appeared to be formed very early on and maintained.

Finally, something needs to be said about the large number of 'undecided', mid-point responses which varied between a fifth and two-thirds of the respondents. This may be seen to indicate a certain lack of interest in the EEC from respondents of this age. Clearly their knowledge of certain EEC functions and regulations is minimal and it may not be easy to observe direct effects of EEC decisions in their daily lives. Hence, many did not express positive or negative attitudes to an institution they knew little of, and cared little about. The Euro-Barometre and other studies have contrasted mainly adult opinions. It would be particularly interesting to consider other European adolescents' conceptions of the EEC and contrast them with these results.

Chapter Six

FOREIGN AND DEVELOPING COUNTRIES

More than ever, young people and their parents and relations travel abroad, particularly on holiday. Figures published every year give some indication of the countries that the British most frequently visit, like Spain, France, and Italy. As one may expect, the countries that most people have been to are either in Europe (which is fairly nearby and therefore comparatively cheap), North America, or other English-speaking countries in the Commonwealth (such as Australia) where they have relations. Without many exceptions these are comparatively rich, industrialized western countries, though some young people have visited countries like Kenya, India, or parts of the West Indies which can be described as developing (or Third World) countries.

Young people, therefore, acquire knowledge about and attitudes to foreign and developing countries through a number of sources: personal experiences of a visit to that country; personal contact with one or more people from that country; the media, particularly newspapers, the radio, and television which frequently feature stories on happenings in other countries; formal education in subjects like history and geography which deal with international affairs; and personal reading which might be motivated by various factors. For all these reasons one may expect young people to be better informed about some countries than others and to associate, correctly or not, particular attributes with certain countries. Famine, political upheaval, and other natural disasters mean that some countries are frequently reported while others are relatively ignored.

Despite the political importance of young people's knowledge of and attitudes to other parts of the world and Britain's relationship with them, very little research has been done in this area. There have been various polls and surveys on British attitudes to foreigners and foreign

73

countries. For instance, a Gallup poll in 1980 on the extent to which foreigners can be trusted revealed interesting findings (Watkins and Worcester 1986). The British nominated the Swiss (72 per cent), Dutch (71 per cent), Americans (70 per cent) highly, the Irish (51 per cent) and Chinese (51 per cent) at least half the time and the Spanish (34 per cent), French (32 per cent), and Russians (18 per cent) least of all. Furthermore, the British felt themselves to be most trustworthy (85 per cent), a higher rating than those they gave to all other European countries. In return the Dutch (75 per cent), Belgians (69 per cent), Danes (66 per cent), Germans (65 per cent), and Irish (63 per cent) felt the British pretty trustworthy, so (overall) did the French (53 per cent). In a study of between fifteen and twenty-four Europeans from each member country of the EEC, it was reported that 58 per cent felt the Americans very or fairly trustworthy while 45 per cent thought the Japanese, 33 per cent the Chinese, and only 16 per cent the Russians to be very or fairly trustworthy.

More recently, the 1985 *British Social Attitudes* survey (Jowell and Witherspoon 1985) reported data on over 1,500 adults' attitudes to international affairs. Excluding the superpowers of America and Russia, the results suggested that only West Germany was thought of as having more influence on world events than the British and then only marginally. Furthermore, compared to Australia, Canada, and China, the respondents felt that British political standing was relatively high. The study also gave the statement: 'The days when Britain was an important world power are over', and 57 per cent agreed, while 26 per cent disagreed. Interestingly, younger people aged 18–24 were less likely to agree (49 per cent) than older people aged 55 and above (61 per cent). The respondents were not very accurate in estimating comparable standards of living — the majority did correctly say that Germany, Canada, and Australia had a higher standard of living, but fewer than half believed this to be true of France and Japan. The respondents were also asked if they thought British interests were better served by closer links with Western Europe (53 per cent), closer links with America (21 per cent), both equally (16 per cent), neither (3 per cent), or don't know (7 per cent).

Over the years, however, various social scientists have done research on such things as world-minded attitudes (Sampson and Smith 1957), the perceptions of nations (Forgas and O'Driscoll 1985), and attitudes to foreign affairs (Christiansen 1959). A number of different theories have been developed to account for people's different beliefs and attitudes to foreign nations and their affairs. For instance, Christiansen has listed six hypotheses about the relationship between personality/individual differences and attitudes towards foreign affairs:

the generalization hypothesis maintains that a person's everyday reaction to conflict/co-operation will be generalized to the international situation;

the latency hypothesis sees an association between the displacement of aggression on to foreign affairs and the extent to which basic impulses are charged with conflict;

the insecurity hypothesis maintains that personal insecurity (fear of the future blocking of personal needs/desires, preferences for national ways of reacting) will affect an individual's attitudes towards foreign affairs;

the nationalism hypothesis contends that a person's attitude towards his/her own nation (pro-, anti-, indifferent) will affect his/her attitude towards foreign affairs;

the knowledge hypothesis suggests that a person's knowledge of international relations (amount and type) will affect his/her attitudes towards foreign affairs;

the channelization hypothesis refers to a number of different viewpoints all having in common the assumption that specific personality traits will have a modifying effect on the relationship between attitudes towards foreign affairs and other personality traits.

But, of course, there are other factors as well as personality which determine a person's attitude to foreign countries. These include education and class (Driver 1963), political/social attitudes, sex, and nationalism (Wish *et al.* 1970).

Interestingly, there is some overlap between dimensions or descriptions emerging from studies which attempt empirically to taxonomize different countries (in terms of their geography, economy, politics, etc.) and studies that examine people's perception of other countries. Typically, a large number of taxonomic factors emerge from empirical studies, such as degree of development, affluence, political orientation, while the sort of dimensions ordinary people use are aggressive/peaceful, communist/capitalist, rich/poor, developed/non-developed, strong/weak, free/oppressed. Sawyer (1967) reported on a study of 236 characteristics of eighty-two nations that wealth, politics, and size were the basic dimensions, while Wish *et al.* (1970) found ordinary people tended to use four dimensions: political alignment, economic development, geography/population, and culture/race. Forgas and O'Driscoll have noted that 'this apparent consensus over time and across cultures regarding the most important features differentiating between countries and peoples is not surprising, given the extremely widespread use of these categories by the media and opinion leaders across different cultures' (Forgas and O'Driscoll 1985: xx).

Nearly all the above work has been done on adults or students and much less on adolescents. There have been some exceptions. For instance, Egan and Nugent (1983) looked at adolescent conceptions of their homeland under the broad headings of cognition/attitude, value systems, political socialization, and self-concept. They proposed four stages which might apply equally to their perception of foreign countries: unreflective attachment (the homeland is seen as a perfect, magical, physical environment); ambivalent attachment (concession that other countries are better than the homeland in certain respects, the entertainment of some negative views held by foreigners); moral evaluation (homeland is thought of in terms of moral and cultural possibilities rather than actualities); and personal identification (the idealistic homeland is identified in terms of personal values and characteristics). They found numerous sex, age, and nationality differences.

In our study we were interested in a number of specific questions.

Experience of foreign countries

To a large extent interest in, attitudes to and knowledge of foreign countries may be thought to be a function of the respondents' experience in foreign countries. Thus, we asked how often they had visited foreign countries, which they would most like to visit, and an estimate of how comparatively rich or poor they thought Britain was compared to all other countries in the world.

Problems facing Britain

It has been suggested that many problems, like unemployment, ensuring sufficient energy, etc., are international rather than simply national problems. That is, what happens in the rest of the world has a marked and crucially important effect on what happens within each individual country. Thus, we asked how important our respondents thought various internationally related problems were.

Predicted developments

Young people are quite naturally orientated towards the future. We were, therefore, interested in how they perceived international affairs over the next ten years in relation to such issues as changes in living standards, the end of famine, and the use of resources.

Friends or foes

It is a very simplistic notion that the various foreign countries in the world could be divided into those seen as friends who merit our help and those seen as foes who were a threat to us. Rather than simply name all or even many different countries in the world, we chose to consider large geo-political areas and ask our respondents whether they believed they were threats or worthy of help.

Knowledge of developing countries

We were particularly interested in the young people's perception of developing countries — how much they knew about them, whether they have ever visited them, and their estimation of the sort of problems that confront them.

Attitudes to developing countries

Finally, we were interested in adolescents' general attitudes to the world's developing countries, treated as a whole. That is, to what extent they believe various stereotypes to be true.

EXPERIENCE OF FOREIGN COUNTRIES

Obviously, one of the most direct ways of getting information about other countries, and one's own, is through travel. We therefore asked our respondents how many times they had visited foreign countries, and more specifically how many times they had been abroad in the last three years. One in four (25 per cent) said that they had never been abroad but one in three (30 per cent) had been four or more times. Eight per cent said they had been abroad ten or more times. There was some indication that males had travelled abroad more frequently than females, though this was only a marginal difference.

Nearly half of our sample (47 per cent) had not been to a foreign country in the past three years but nearly one in five (18 per cent) had been three or more times. Again, there was a minor sex difference, this time indicating that females had travelled more frequently than males. More males (40 per cent) than females (34 per cent) had *never* been abroad.

Although we did not ask our respondents which country they *had* been to, we did ask them to indicate from a list of twenty countries which country they would most *like* to visit. The most popular by a long way, and that nominated by nearly a third (32 per cent) of the respondents, was America. The second and joint third nominations were also English-speaking countries and part of the Commonwealth — namely, Australia (14 per cent) and Canada (9 per cent). Spain (9 per cent) and Greece (8 per cent) were the next most popularly nominated destinations, with all the rest receiving between 1 and 4 per cent. The influence of American TV programmes, relatives, past travel experience could each in turn and together account for these findings.

As we were going to ask questions about Third World and developing countries, we thought it a good idea that we establish how rich or poor our respondents thought Britain was compared to other countries. Although 11 per cent placed Britain on the poor side of the seven-point scale, 14 per cent said they did not know and 24 per cent put Britain on the mid-point, the majority (52 per cent) placed Britain, quite correctly, on the rich side of the poor/rich continuum. No doubt this perception has some impact on how respondents perceived other countries.

PROBLEMS FACING BRITAIN

The perception of the problems facing foreign countries is no doubt influenced by the perception of problems facing one's own country and vice versa. Hence, we started out by asking respondents how important or unimportant they rated nine problems facing Britain. The order of importance as shown in table 6.1 was thus: reducing

Table 6.1 Problems facing Britain

How important are the following problems facing Britain?

		All %	Sex Male %	Female %	10-14 %	Age 15-16 %	17 + %
1. Reducing the differences between regions of our country by helping the less developed or those most in need	Very important	23	20	25	24	21	23
	Important	48	48	47	46	48	48
	Of little importance	23	24	22	22	25	23
	Not important	7	8	6	8	6	6
2. Ensuring non-nuclear energy supplies (e.g. coal, oil) are maintained	Very important	40	40	42	45	36	41
	Important	39	39	41	39	42	38
	Of little importance	14	12	13	10	16	14
	Not important	7	9	4	6	6	7
3. Try and reduce the number both of very rich and very poor people	Very important	26	26	25	21	24	33
	Important	36	35	38	37	36	35
	Of little importance	29	28	30	30	32	24
	Not important	9	11	7	12	8	8
4. Fighting against terrorism	Very important	56	58	56	58	55	61
	Important	31	29	32	32	31	30
	Of little importance	8	8	8	8	10	8
	Not important	5	5	4	2	4	1
5. Helping poor countries in Africa, Asia, and South America	Very important	42	35	50	53	40	32
	Important	37	40	36	33	39	42
	Of little importance	14	16	11	9	15	17
	Not important	7	9	3	5	6	9
6. Reducing unemployment	Very important	78	76	79	72	82	80
	Important	17	19	16	20	15	17
	Of little importance	3	3	2	4	2	3
	Not important	2	2	3	4	1	0
7. Defend our interests against the super-powers such as USA and Soviet Union	Very important	34	40	28	32	37	32
	Important	40	37	43	39	40	41
	Of little importance	20	16	22	22	18	18
	Not important	6	7	7	7	5	9
8. Protecting nature and fighting pollution	Very important	42	44	39	44	39	43
	Important	41	37	44	36	42	43
	Of little importance	14	13	14	15	15	10
	Not important	4	6	3	5	4	4
9. Strengthen our military defence against possible enemies	Very important	30	31	28	30	31	28
	Important	41	40	44	46	39	40
	Of little importance	20	19	21	17	22	22
	Not important	8	10	7	7	8	10

unemployment (95 per cent), fighting terrorism (87 per cent), helping poor countries (79 per cent), ensuring non-nuclear energy supplies (79 per cent), defending our interests against the superpowers (74 per cent), strengthening our military defences (71 per cent), reducing economic differences between regions (71 per cent) and reducing the number of very rich and very poor people (62 per cent). Thus, all the problems were considered important and fewer than 10 per cent of the respondents said any of the problems was not important, though nearly a third (29 per cent) thought it of little importance that Britain 'try and reduce the number both of very rich people and very poor people' and a fifth thought it of little importance to 'defend our interests against the superpowers such as the USA and Soviet Union' and 'strengthen our military defence against possible enemies'.

Many of the items showed sex differences. More females than males believed it is important to reduce the differences between regions of the country and to help poor countries but less important to defend British interests against superpowers and strengthen military defences. There were also a number of age-related differences, though not all of these were linear. Three of the largest differences indicated that as adolescents get older they feel it is more important to reduce the numbers of very rich and very poor and to reduce unemployment, but less important to help poor countries. Presumably as they get older adolescents become aware of different sorts of economic, political, and social issues which they perceive as problems facing the country.

It would have been interesting to ask respondents to speculate on the extent to which these nine problems occurred in other developed and underdeveloped countries or indeed to know whether adolescents from other countries perceived the problems facing Britain as the same as those chosen by the adolescents in our sample.

PREDICTED DEVELOPMENTS

Youth is frequently future-oriented so we asked our respondents which of six major developments they believed might or might not occur in the next ten years. Three questions showed a roughly two-thirds/one-third split. About two in three did *not* think international tensions would be lessened or that the difference in standards of living between rich and poor countries would be reduced but they did believe that the world's resources would be used more thoughtfully in the interests of future generations. Nearly three out of four, however, were optimistic that in the next ten years progress in science and technology will have allowed us to improve the situation of the poorest countries. There was less agreement over two final questions, with slightly fewer than half believing that famine would be lessened and more mutual confidence and trust between developed and underdeveloped countries would occur.

Although there were no significant sex or class differences, there were consistent and dramatic linear age differences on every question. Compared to the youngest group, the oldest group believed it *less* likely that international tensions would be reduced, differences in living standards between rich and poor countries would decrease, famine would be lessened, and there would be more mutual confidence and trust between developed countries. Older respondents were also less optimistic about progress in science and technology helping poorest countries and world resources being more thoughtfully used.

Overall, the pattern that emerges is that British adolescents are relatively pessimistic about the future and that as they get older they tend to become less rather than more optimistic — perhaps one might argue more realistic. Areas of optimism are, however, apparent with respect to science and technology and to a lesser extent conservation.

Table 6.2 Predicted developments in ten years

How do you think things will develop in our world over the next ten years or so?

		All %	Age 10-14 %	15-16 %	17 + %
1.	International tensions will have lessened	33	45	39	28
2.	The difference in standards of living between the industrial countries and the poorer countries will have become smaller	38	49	45	30
3.	Famine will have lessened throughout the world	42	49	47	30
4.	Progress in science and technology will have allowed us to improve the situation of the poorest countries	72	79	74	64
5.	There will be more mutual confidence and trust between the developed countries and the other countries than there is at present	47	50	47	42
6.	The world's resources will be used more thoughtfully in the interest of future generations	62	74	72	70

Note: Percentages are of those who agreed with each item.

FRIENDS OR FOES

Which countries should Britain be helping and which are a threat? It may be argued that helping and threat are not opposites and that, just because a country does not merit being helped, it does not necessarily mean that it is a threat. However, we decided to follow the format of the questionnaire used in the Euro-Barometre so as to compare adult with adolescent responses.

Over 90 per cent of the sample said that we should be helping African countries, 70 per cent thought that we should be helping India and Pakistan, and 69 per cent countries in south east Asia. But 70 per cent also thought we should be helping all European countries and 65 per cent specifically West European countries or conversely that these did not present themselves as a threat. Over three-quarters saw Japan and America as threats, presumably from an economic point of view. As one may predict, the country that fewest respondents wished to help (14 per cent) and most saw as a threat (86 per cent) was Russia (and other Eastern bloc countries).

Table 6.3 Perceptions of countries that we should be helping

	Total %	Sex Male %	Sex Female %	Age 10-14 %	Age 15-16 %	Age 17 + %
Africa	92	91	94	94	92	90
South America	58	56	60	55	59	61
India and Pakistan	70	71	69	65	72	74
Japan	30	33	26	24	32	35
North America	33	37	27	29	33	37
Middle East	37	35	41	41	40	31
Russia (and other Eastern bloc countries)	14	15	12	12	13	15
European countries	70	69	70	66	68	76
Western European countries	65	66	71	66	70	68
South East Asia	69	66	71	66	70	68
China	45	46	44	42	45	49

There were numerous sex and age differences, with females favouring more than males that Britain help Africa, South America, the Middle East, and south east Asia, but feeling less than males that Britain should help Japan and North America. Age differences were also very noticeable. Compared to the youngest group, the oldest group of adolescents was less eager to help African countries and the Middle East but more interested in helping South American countries, India and Pakistan, Japan, North America, and Europe.

It should be pointed out that respondents were asked to indicate either those countries which Britain should help or those which, in one way or another, are a threat to us. The threat therefore could be seen as social, political, economic, military, etc. Thus, whereas one country could be seen to be a major military threat but a minor economic threat and another a major economic threat but a minor military threat, they could still receive the same score. It is, therefore, probably more useful to consider the helping rather than the threat data.

KNOWLEDGE OF DEVELOPING COUNTRIES

In a series of ten questions we attempted to ascertain what our sample knew of developing countries. Over 60 per cent said that they had thought either a lot or quite a lot about developing countries in Africa, Asia, and South America, while over a third admitted to having done so very little. More females than males and younger rather than older children claimed to have thought a lot about developing countries.

We were particularly interested in the extent to which our respondents learnt about developing countries from the media in general. Nearly three-quarters of our sample (71 per cent) reported that they had seen or heard something about developing countries in the media. Many more older (78 per cent) than younger (64 per cent) reported this presumably because of the range and extent of media to which they exposed themselves. Asked whether the media in general give too much, too little, or about the right amount of exposure to developing countries, a third (31 per cent) thought too little and under half (44 per cent) about the right amount. Females and the youngest group of adolescents were more satisfied with the status quo while older respondents more than younger adolescents wanted more information. Third, we asked whether our sample felt the media present a fair picture of the situation in developing countries. About half thought the picture fair (52 per cent), a quarter unfair (26 per cent) and a quarter did not know (22 per cent). There were no sex or age differences on this question.

Once again we asked our sample whether they were in favour of helping developing countries as a whole and nearly 90 per cent said they were, though of course the precise nature of the help was not specified. Females were more keen to help than males and younger respondents more keen than older respondents.

Table 6.4 Developing countries

		All %	Male %	Female %	10-14 %	15-16 %	17+ %
1.	How much have you thought about the problems of poorer (developing, Third World) countries such as those in Africa, South America, Asia before? Have you thought about them a lot, quite a lot, a little, or almost never?	A lot	21	17	25	22	20	20
		Quite a lot	41	40	42	46	42	35
		A little	28	31	26	24	30	32
		Almost never	10	12	7	8	8	13
2.	Have you recently seen or heard in papers, or on radio, or on television, anything about developing countries?	Yes	71	71	70	64	72	78
		No	15	16	15	18	14	13
		Don't know	14	13	15	18	14	9
3.	Would you say that newspapers, radio, and television give too much information about the situation in the developing countries, too little information, or about the right amount?	Too much	14	19	10	13	14	17
		Too little	31	30	31	25	32	37
		Right amount	44	40	47	48	45	37
		Don't know	11	11	12	14	9	9
4.	In your opinion are we given a fair picture or not of the situation in the developing countries?	Fair picture	52	52	52	52	55	50
		Unfair picture	26	25	26	23	24	30
		Don't know	22	23	22	25	21	20
5.	Some people favour, others are against helping the developing countries. Where do you personally stand on these issues?	For helping	30	25	35	33	28	28
		Some help	58	58	58	55	59	60
		Against help	8	11	4	7	8	9
		Strongly against	4	6	3	5	5	3

But what experience did our sample have of developing countries? We asked them, 'besides what you have been able to read in the newspapers or see on television, what personal experience have you had of developing countries?' Fourteen per cent said they had visited these countries as a tourist. Thirteen per cent said they had or have friends or acquaintances among people coming from other countries. Five per cent said they had lived in a developing country or had visited one but not as a tourist. In all, 57 per cent claimed to have no real personal experience of these countries and would, therefore, have to base their attitudes on what they had read, seen, or heard.

We then asked, 'would you say that in the part of the country where you live, there are a lot, some, a few or no people who come from developing countries living there?' As regards contact with immigrants from developing countries, 10 per cent of our sample said there were a lot in their area, 17 per cent some, 31 per cent a few, and 20 per cent none, which probably reflects the fact that the sample was drawn from throughout the British Isles where the distribution of the migrant populations is highly uneven. Twenty per cent said they did not know.

The next question asked whether they felt that in the next 10–15 years what happens in developing countries, their political situation, their economies, their population growth, will in some way affect our lives in Britain. Nearly half (48 per cent) of our sample thought that what happened in developing countries would affect their lives in Britain with just over a third (35 per cent) claiming not to know. Males (50 per cent) more than females (45 per cent) and older (57 per cent) more than younger (40 per cent) respondents felt that Britain would experience the effects of changes in the developing world.

We then asked which of four types of countries we should be helping most — the poorest, those on which we depend for raw materials, those which buy a lot of products from us, or those which are of strategic interest for political or defence reasons. The vast majority considered their need (i.e., the poorest — 74 per cent) above Britain's strategic interests in terms of raw materials (11 per cent), markets (9 per cent), or political/defence strategic reasons (6 per cent). However, males more than females (4 per cent), and older respondents (7 per cent) more than younger respondents placed more importance on strategic interests, though still over two-thirds placed poverty as the single most important criterion meriting help. A final question tested the perceived benevolence more closely in that we asked to what extent Britain should continue helping the Third World even if it cost more because of lack of growth. The largest number (37 per cent) favoured decreasing help when your own standards of living stopped increasing, but a similar number (34 per cent) believed Britain should continue even under those conditions. Only 14 per cent said help should be stopped under these conditions and a similar number (14 per cent) said that they didn't know. Females (35 per cent) more than males (33 per cent) and older (36 per cent) more than younger (32 per cent) adolescents were in favour of decreasing help to developing countries if the British standard of living had stopped rising.

ATTITUDES TO DEVELOPING COUNTRIES

Finally, we asked for reactions to fifteen general statements about their attitudes to developing countries as a whole. These statements reflect the opinions about issues frequently mentioned when Third World issues and the status of developing countries are mentioned.

Nearly three-quarters (72 per cent) and more females (84 per cent) than males (70 per cent) believed the developing countries suffer from an unfavourable climate despite the tourist industry of these countries presenting them as having ideal climates. In all, 40 per cent agreed that a legacy of colonialism had held back their development and a similar number expressed no opinion about it. Less than half (43 per cent) thought they were exploited by developed countries but again a fairly large number (35 per cent) expressed no opinion, presumably because they had little information on this issue.

Most of the sample (56 per cent) disagreed with the frequently levelled claim that developing peoples do not really want to work. Females (57 per cent) more than males (52 per cent) and older (59 per cent) more than younger (49 per cent) people disagreed with this item. But the vast majority (77 per cent) of our sample did believe that their populations were growing too fast. Males (75 per cent) more than females (67 per cent) and older (79 per cent) more than younger (70 per cent) children agreed that this was a major problem.

Almost exactly two-thirds (66 per cent) felt that most developing countries had not managed to achieve stable government. Many more older (69 per cent) compared to younger (57 per cent) respondents agreed with this statement. A very similar pattern emerged from the statement concerning corruption in developing countries. Sixty per cent agreed and more older (71 per cent) than younger (55 per cent) respondents agreed that a rich minority exploits the rest of the population.

Over half the sample (51 per cent) did not express an opinion as to whether developing countries were happier as colonies though there was a tendency for younger adolescents to believe this to be more true than older adolescents.

The sample was split almost exactly three ways over the issue of whether Third World, developing countries were beginning to compete with British products. There was some indication that younger respondents believed this more (40 per cent) than older respondents (33 per cent) though precisely where they get this information is highly uncertain.

More than four out of ten (44 per cent) and more females (53 per cent) than males (48 per cent) thought that Britain had a moral duty to help developing countries. Much the same number (47 per cent) agreed that developing countries face problems which European countries took centuries to overcome, though over a third expressed no opinion on this issue.

Table 6.5 Attitudes to developing countries

	Agree %	Neither %	Disagree %
They suffer from an unfavourable climate	72	20	8
In former times the fact that they were colonies held back their development	40	40	20
They are exploited by the developed countries such as our own	43	35	22
They do not really want to work	24	20	56
Their populations are growing too fast	77	15	8
They have not managed to achieve stable government	66	26	8
A rich minority exploits the rest of the population	60	27	13
They were happier when they were colonies	31	51	18
They are beginning to compete with us with their own products	33	34	33
We have a moral duty to help them	44	30	26
They face problems which European countries have taken centuries to overcome	47	39	14
It is in our interests to help them	57	23	20
No matter what is done to help them they will never succeed in escaping from their situation of poverty	45	25	30
They must be encouraged to develop their own way rather than try to imitate us	64	23	13
We British also have a lot to learn from the people of these countries	48	29	23

Fifty-seven per cent of the sample believed it was in the British interest to help developing countries though fewer males (53 per cent) than females (60 per cent) and fewer older (49 per cent) than younger people (51 per cent) believed this. In fact, there was some indication of fatalism in our respondents as nearly half (45 per cent) agreed that no matter what help they receive most developing countries will not escape their situation of poverty. But our sample were not very chauvinistic as about two-thirds (64 per cent) believed developing countries should not imitate Britain but go their own way. In fact nearly half (48 per cent) believed that the British have a lot to learn from people in developing countries. More older than younger (57 per cent vs. 42 per cent) respondents believed this and more females than males (57 per cent vs. 47 per cent).

Overall, these results are not very dissimilar from those of adults and reveal a certain amount of compassion (and ignorance) about the problems facing developing countries and the extent to which Britain and other developed countries should be assisting them.

CONCLUDING REMARKS

Our sample appeared relatively pessimistic about the future and the sort of problems facing Britain and indeed the world over the next ten years. Nevertheless, they seemed reasonably well informed about and compassionate towards the Third World.

In our study we were unable either to ask detailed questions concerning the respondents' factual knowledge about developing countries or to focus on the particular issues of individual countries. Hence, these results are presented at a fairly general level which may mean that these attitudes and beliefs are not very predictive of future behaviour.

By and large, our respondents claimed to be interested in and to have thought about developing countries and seemed satisfied that the information they received about them on the media was sufficient and fair. Despite the fact that few had had any direct experience of developing countries or of people who came from them, they were in general in favour of helping them, particularly the poorest. Older respondents were more keen to help countries that had some strategic usefulness and less eager to help if it meant it cost more to Britain.

The sort of problems that our adolescents saw developing countries as having were poor climates, too rapidly growing populations, and unstable governments, and to a lesser extent a rich minority exploiting the rest. Many did not express opinions about the effects of colonialization, the speed of their development, or their potential economic threat, but most did not believe that they were lazy. The majority thought that as a whole they merited help, should be encouraged to do things their own way, and that Britain could learn something from their experience.

There were a number of sex and age differences, but few class differences. Though there were inconsistencies, it seemed that older children (17 +) rather than younger children (10–14) and males more than females were pragmatic and conservative while the latter tended to be more idealistic. Certainly, from the 'don't know' or 'neither agree nor disagree' scores, it seemed the case that our sample had opinions on many of these issues even if they were not particularly well informed about them.

Chapter Seven

THE ROLE OF MEN AND WOMEN

A great deal of our behaviour is controlled by socially and culturally approved norms of conduct and beliefs about one's own sex. In all societies certain characteristics and behaviours are traditionally associated with and deemed appropriate for men and for women. Socialization practices instil these social mores in individuals from a very early age. And they can become permanent ingredients of the person's psychological make-up and outlook on the world.

The emergence of the women's rights movement during the 1970s brought to light extremes of sex-stereotyping which characterized beliefs about the appropriate roles for women. According to some commentators these stereotypes actively restricted the range of opportunities and prospects that are available to women compared with those for men, particularly in professional and occupational spheres. Social injustices against women were being fed by prevailing sex-stereotypes which no longer had a place in modern industrial society.

Sex stereotypes are developed during childhood so we should expect them to show themselves among teenagers and young adults. However, there have been some improvements in the occupational prospects of women in recent years, even though there is plenty of scope still for further improvement. Media models of independent, career-minded women have emerged together with success stories about women in business. But how far have these developments spread to other areas of social behaviour and to beliefs about what women should or should not do with their lives?

There is some evidence that, despite a substantial increase in women's employment during the 1950s, 1960s, and early 1970s, little change occurred in the allocation of household tasks between men and women during the same period. Household cleaning, washing dishes, and shopping were still seen essentially as things done by the wife (Duncan *et al.* 1973). Indeed, shopping was found to be more exclusively the wife's job in 1971 than in 1955, while household repairs remained principally the duty of the husband.

This American research served as a model for more recent British surveys. From the 1984 survey of *British Social Attitudes*, respondents were given a list of eight household tasks. Married respondents were asked how they actually shared each task with their partners. Unmarried respondents were asked how they thought each task *should* be shared (Airey 1984). The findings suggested that husbands rarely played the major role in most everyday and time-consuming household jobs, such as the cleaning, cooking, or washing and ironing. They played a slightly larger role in household shopping, in decisions about decorating, and in washing dishes. But they only came into their own in household repairs. According to this survey, however, single people (those who had never been married) would arrange things differently; the majority of this group favoured equal participation by men and women in doing household chores generally. The formerly married (who were not living with a partner) were less egalitarian than the single people, but more so than married couples were in their actual allocation of tasks.

The same questions were repeated in the 1985 *British Social Attitudes* survey. Witherspoon (1985) reported that 87 per cent of married women said they were mainly responsible for general domestic duties in the household, and 7 per cent said they shared responsibility with their spouse; 75 per cent of married men said that their spouse was responsible for these jobs, while 14 per cent claimed to share responsibility with their partner. When asked who was responsible for general care of the children in the household, 76 per cent of married women with children said they were mainly responsible and 14 per cent said that they shared responsibility with their husbands. Among married men with children 72 per cent said their spouse was mainly responsible for looking after the children, and 21 per cent said that caring for the children was shared.

On the question of who should do various household chores, married men and women gave remarkably similar answers — in both cases favouring a more equal division of labour than actually existed. But the answers for both sexes were still far from egalitarian and reflected traditional stereotypes. Ideals were clearly tempered by current experience and married men and women were less egalitarian than either the formerly married or single people who had never been married.

The 1985 *British Social Attitudes* survey suggested that, while there was widespread disapproval of formal obstacles to women's equality and of overt discrimination, there was much less evidence of attitude change in respect of the domestic division of labour which is a major cause of labour market inequality. Some real changes have been brought about by legally providing for equality of opportunity; others have been brought about by improvements in employment opportunities for part-time workers. And yet it seems probable that, in the absence of changes in attitude and behaviour at home regarding who does the household chores, women will continue to be faced with problems of employment and occupational success outside the home that are not so often experienced by men.

The survey asked all employees whether they thought of their work as mainly men's work, mainly women's work, or work that either men or women can do. The responses indicated that men were significantly more likely to describe their work as mainly men's work than women were to describe theirs as mainly women's work.

In our survey, we asked young people for their opinions concerning the role of women in marital and family contexts, in occupational and work contexts, in politics, and in other social situations. We also probed their opinions about sexual relationships, the roles of husband and wife in marriage, and finally about perceived causes of marital unhappiness.

BELIEFS ABOUT WOMEN, MARRIAGE AND FAMILY

Five attitude statements were used to investigate what young people felt about the rights and role of women in marital and family contexts. We return to this general area again later when we consider beliefs about appropriate husband and wife roles in the marriage relationship.

The attitudes expressed indicated that young people today are in favour of a sharing of household responsibilities between the sexes and of women having equality with men in contexts in which, more traditionally, men would be expected to have the upper hand. More than three out of four young people interviewed here (79 per cent) believed that if a woman goes out to work, then her husband should share the housework. This was extensively endorsed by youth of both sexes, though perhaps not unexpectedly, more often by females (86 per cent) than by males (70 per cent). Both sexes were agreed to an extent

75 per cent), however, that a woman should be as free as a man to propose marriage.

In the traditional marriage ceremony, the vows made by the woman embody a more extreme commitment than those made by the man, in so far as the woman has to propose to 'love, honour and *obey*' her husband, while the husband only promises to 'love and honour' his wife, without any promise to obey her. A majority of young respondents (58 per cent) felt that this was an insult to a woman. This belief was the most prevalent among both sexes, though more so among females (66 per cent) than males (48 per cent).

Beliefs about the relationships of the mother and father in the context of child-raising were less clear-cut. On balance more young people disagreed than agreed that the father should have more authority than the mother in bringing up children (49 per cent against 26 per cent) or that it should be the woman who decides how many children a couple has (41 per cent against 25 per cent). There was a pronounced sex difference on the first of these two items, however. Females (58 per cent) were much more likely than males (38 per cent) to reject this proposition.

WOMEN AND WORK

These days more and more women contemplate not just going out to work but also having careers. There are still social pressures placed on women to restrict themselves to marriage and family life. And even those who choose to pursue a profession may find themselves discriminated against because of their sex.

Witherspoon (1985) reported that adult attitudes towards women, work, and marriage showed signs of leaning towards egalitarianism rather than traditionalism. There was mainly disagreement with the opinion that 'a wife should avoid earning more than her husband' (rejected by 57 per cent), while few (14 per cent) accepted it). Similarly, a narrow majority (52 per cent) agreed that 'more women should enter politics'.

In the same survey, more respondents agreed than disagreed that 'it is wrong for mothers of young children to go out to work' (42 per cent versus 32 per cent), while disagreement outweighed agreement on views such as 'children are essential for a happy marriage' (29 per cent versus 41 per cent) and 'it should be the women who decide how many children a couple has' (27 per cent versus 42 per cent).

Some traditional beliefs and attitudes die hard, but, with the development of the new breed of professionally ambitious women and a world in which horizons have opened up for the professionally or work-orientated female, some shifts in viewpoint can be optimistically interpreted. And it is among the young, rather than the old, where open-mindedness might be expected to occur. So what do young people today feel about women and work?

Ten statements were used to investigate youth attitudes concerning women and work. The general picture to emerge was one which reflected endorsement of equal opportunities for women in the workplace and the belief that women were suited to work (as well as have families) and had as much to offer as did men in the occupational sphere.

A large majority (78 per cent) believed that women should have completely equal opportunities with men in getting jobs and beng promoted. Females (83 per cent) were more often in agreement with this point of view than were males (70 per cent). There was widespread belief also that women were better off having their own jobs and the freedom that would bring (60 per cent). Once again this sort of belief was much more prevalent among females (67 per cent) than among males (50 per cent).

On the ability of women to do a good job, or at least to be as capable as men, opinions were mixed and differed between the sexes. Over half our youth respondents overall (55 per cent) agreed that there are many jobs a man can do better than a woman, though males (67 per cent) believed this much more often than females (46 per cent). Fewer overall (39 per cent) thought that women generally handle positions of responsibility better than men do, especially among males (27 per cent) but much less among females (48 per cent). On the same theme, however, there was widespread disagreement that women should not be bosses in important jobs in business and industry (61 per cent) and that women have less to offer than men in the world of business and industry (55 per cent). In each case, though, females were much more likely than males to reject these opinions. The weight of opinions across youth generally indicated that women ought not to allow being married or having a family to restrict their occupational aspirations, though this was not without exception. Most respondents (62 per cent) rejected the view that a woman's place is in the home looking after her family rather than following a career of her own. This opinion was nowhere near as commonplace among male youth (46 per cent) as among female

Table 7.1 Women and work

	All %	Male %	Female %	10-14 %	15-16 %	17 + %
		Sex			*Age*	
Women should have completely equal opportunities in getting jobs and promotion with men						
Agree	78	70	83	71	73	86
Neither	13	15	12	17	15	8
Disagree	9	16	5	12	11	7
Women are better off having their own jobs and freedom to do as they please rather than being treated like a lady in the old-fashioned way						
Agree	60	50	67	61	55	63
Neither	24	29	20	20	29	23
Disagree	16	21	13	20	16	15
There are many jobs that men can do better than women						
Agree	55	67	46	54	53	59
Neither	18	18	19	16	20	18
Disagree	27	15	36	31	26	23
It is wrong for mothers of small children to go out to work						
Agree	50	58	44	53	51	48
Neither	23	20	26	26	23	21
Disagree	26	23	30	22	26	31
Women generally handle positions of responsibility better than men do						
Agree	39	27	48	57	34	29
Neither	39	39	40	31	39	47
Disagree	22	35	12	12	28	25
Women should worry less about being equal with men and more about becoming good wives and mothers						
Agree	38	47	30	47	37	31
Neither	21	23	21	20	22	22
Disagree	41	30	48	33	42	47
Women have less to offer than men in the world of business and industry						
Agree	24	31	14	31	25	19
Neither	21	24	18	28	21	14
Disagree	55	45	68	41	55	67
Women should not be bosses in important jobs in business and industry						
Agree	21	27	16	28	20	13
Neither	18	25	14	25	15	20
Disagree	61	48	70	47	65	67

95

Table 7.1 (cont.)

	All %	Sex Male %	Sex Female %	Age 10-14 %	Age 15-16 %	Age 17+ %
A woman's place is in the home looking after her family rather than following a career of her own						
Agree	20	29	14	27	21	15
Neither	18	25	12	22	16	16
Disagree	62	46	74	50	64	69
A wife should avoid earning more than her husband does						
Agree	17	22	13	20	21	10
Neither	22	27	19	28	19	21
Disagree	61	51	69	53	61	69

youth (74 per cent), however. There was also widespread belief that a wife should not mind earning more than her husband (61 per cent), again endorsed more by females (69 per cent) than males (51 per cent). There was a less clearly defined viewpoint on the relative merits of women concentrating on becoming good wives and mothers rather than worrying about being equal with men. There was little difference in the extent of agreement or disagreement with this item overall, though males (47 per cent) agreed more often than females (30 per cent) that women should focus on marriage and family matters. Mothers should, it seems, exhibit a degree of responsibility when they have young children. Thus, half the respondents agreed that it is wrong for mothers of very small children to go out to work.

WOMEN: EDUCATION AND TRAINING

Should women be encouraged to aim for occupational or professional jobs when they are young? Two out of three respondents (65 per cent) thought that daughters should receive as much encouragement as sons from their families to go to college in search of higher education. Even more (76 per cent) felt that girls should have as much opportunity to do apprenticeships and learn as boys. There were marked sex differences in extent of agreement with the last opinion, however. Females (83 per cent) were much more likely than males (67 per cent) to agree with it. Respondents aged 17 + years (74 per cent) were more likely than those aged 15-16 (56 per cent) or 12-14 (25 per cent) to agree that daughters should be encouraged to stay on at school and go to college as much as sons.

WOMEN AND POLITICS

Women politicians throughout the world have become much more prominent in the last few years. Is this phenomenon reflected in any way in young people's opinions about the acceptability of women being in politics. On the whole, opinions concerning women in politics were favourable, especially among female respondents. Yet only two out of three young people felt that more women should enter politics (65 per cent) and that there should be more women leaders in important jobs in public life, such as politics (62 per cent). Substantial and predictable sex differences appeared. Females (76 per cent) were much more likely than males (50 per cent) to agree that more women should enter politics. Females (73 per cent) were also more likely than males (47 per cent) to say there should be more women leaders in important jobs in public life such as politics.

WOMEN AND SOCIAL BEHAVIOUR

Outside the professional educational spheres certain behaviours are traditionally expected of men and women in social contexts. Do young people specify decent codes of social practice for women? In general, our youth sample felt that the female sex should enjoy pretty much the same social freedom as males. Most (72 per cent) felt that girls should be allowed to stay out late just as much as boys. Females (77 per cent) were more likely to say this than males (64 per cent). Most (69 per cent) also felt that women should be able to go everywhere a man goes, including going into pubs alone. Females (76 per cent) held this opinion more often than males (62 per cent). There was a consistent age trend. Older children aged 17 + (77 per cent) were much more likely than the youngest (10–14s) (59 per cent) to feel that a woman should be able to go everywhere a man does.

Most of both sexes agreed, however, that it does sound worse when a woman swears than when a man does (68 per cent). But respondents aged 17 + (90 per cent) were more likely to agree with this than younger 10–16s (63 per cent). Opinions were less consistent when it came to the telling of dirty jokes. Females (52 per cent) were more likely than males (39 per cent) to feel that it is all right for women to

tell them just as much as it is for men. Older respondents aged 17 +
(27 per cent) less often felt this was appropriate than did younger
respondents aged 10–14 years (35 per cent).

Going Dutch on dates, especially when girls earn as much as their
boyfriends, was very widely favoured (by 59 per cent). Again there
were sex and age differences. Males (62 per cent) believed more often
than did females (56 per cent) that girls earning as much as their
boyfriends should pay for themselves when going out with them. The
older respondents aged 17 + (68 per cent) were more likely to agree
with this than younger ones (53 per cent). And, finally, most
adolescents (63 per cent) felt that women should be able to have sex
before marriage. Females (78 per cent) were more in favour of this
than were males (56 per cent), however.

ATTITUDES ABOUT SEX MATTERS

It is during adolescence when most individuals first become sexually
aware and have their earliest sexual experience. We wanted to examine
the attitudes of young people today towards sex and sexual relations.
Do they find certain types of sexual relationships or behaviour acceptable and others less so?

In the supposedly permissive society which grew up during the 1960s
and 1970s, values about sexuality and sexual behaviour changed so
that a greater range and variety of viewpoints were openly expressed.
Prominent among these changes were greater public acceptability of
sexual relations outside marriage, of having many sexual partners, and
of sexual relations between members of the same sex.

But how open-minded are the youth of today about these matters?
Do they believe that society should be permissive of all types of sexual
relationships? Should sexual relations be restricted to marriage
partners? Should sex be for pleasure or only or mainly for having
children? These and other opinions were asked of the youth sample
surveyed here.

The 1984 survey of *British Social Attitudes* found, for example, that
just 16 per cent of people in this country felt that pre-marital sexual
relationships are wrong, while 42 per cent felt they were not wrong
at all. People were less permissive, however, with respect to adulterous
relationships. Fifty-eight per cent thought that extra-marital relationships were always wrong, with a further 25 per cent saying they were
mostly wrong (Jowell and Airey 1984).

Table 7.2 Beliefs about sex matters

	All %	*Sex* Male %	Female %	*Age* 10–14 %	15–16 %	17 + %
I feel that society should permit only heterosexual (male/female) relationships	18	18	18	27	13	14
I feel that society should be permissive of all types of sexual relationships	48	45	50	44	53	48
I prefer not to answer this question	34	37	32	30	34	37
I feel that a person should engage in sexual relations only after he or she is married	14	13	16	20	13	10
I approve of premarital sex	73	73	74	64	77	78
I prefer not to answer this question	13	14	11	16	10	12
I feel that the institution of marriage, as we know it today, should be here to stay	21	18	23	21	21	21
I feel that the institution of marriage, as we know it today, should be abolished	16	16	17	22	16	22
I prefer not to answer this question	63	66	60	57	63	67
I feel that the main reason for having sexual relations should be to have children	22	16	26	27	17	23
I feel that having sexual relations for pleasure only is fine	67	70	64	59	71	69
I prefer not to answer this question	12	14	10	14	12	8
I feel that children should not be aware of the fact that their parents engage in sexual relations until the parents feel it is necessary to introduce the subject	16	15	17	19	19	11
I feel it is all right for children of any age to be aware of the fact that their parents engage in sexual relations	52	48	55	60	46	54
I prefer not to answer this question	32	36	28	21	35	36

Note: Percentages indicate the extent to which respondents *agreed* with each statement.

Pre-marital sex has become increasingly accepted. Donnell (1979) concluded that the traditional idea of marriage as a precondition of sexual relations is disappearing. She found, among a sample of women who had married in the late 1950s, that 35 per cent reported having sexual relationships with their husbands before marriage. Among women who had married in the early 1970s, however, the proportion was 74 per cent.

Opinions concerning pre-marital sex, however, do vary with age. Airey and Brook (1986) reported that just 7 per cent of 18–34-year-olds in a national survey sample agreed that sex before marriage is always or mostly wrong, compared with 19 per cent of 35–54-year-olds and 45 per cent of those aged over 55 years.

On the opinions of the types of sexual relationships which should be permitted, fewer than one in five young people (18 per cent) said they felt that only heterosexual (male-female) relationships should be permitted. Nearly half (48 per cent) were in favour of accepting all types of sexual relationships. One in three (34 per cent), however, preferred not to give an opinion.

A large majority (73 per cent) approved of premarital sex, while few (14 per cent) thought that a person should engage in sexual relations only after he or she is married. Two out of three (67 per cent) felt that having sex for pleasure only is fine, and just one in five (22 per cent) felt that the main reason for having sexual relations should be to have children. Most (63 per cent) would not be drawn on the question of whether marriage should be abolished or not, however. Around one in five (21 per cent) felt that marriage, as an institution, should be here to stay.

Few (16 per cent) felt that parents should be prudent with their children about the fact that they may engage in sexual relations with each other. Over half (52 per cent) felt that it is all right for children of any age to know that their parents have this sort of relationship.

OPINIONS ABOUT THE ROLES OF HUSBAND AND WIFE

At the beginning of this chapter, we mentioned findings from surveys of *British Social Attitudes* in 1984 and 1985 which reported a marked division of labour among husbands and wives in the doing of domestic chores. Among single people who had never been married, however, on the questions of how domestic chores should be allocated, there was a strong feeling that both partners should share general household duties equally. What do adolescents feel about who should take responsibility for domestic chores?

On a subject related both to marriage and sex roles, a series of attitudes towards the roles of husband and wife were examined. In connection with different kinds of housework, should the job be done mainly by the man, mainly by the woman, or by both equally?

Table 7.3 Beliefs about the roles of husband and wife

	All %	Sex Male %	Female %	10–14 %	Age 15–16 %	17 + %
Deciding what colour to decorate the living room						
By both equally	77	75	79	74	71	86
Mainly by the woman	16	17	15	20	19	10
Mainly by the man	7	9	6	6	11	4
Doing the shopping						
By both equally	68	60	74	62	65	75
Mainly by the woman	30	36	25	34	32	24
Mainly by the man	3	4	1	4	3	1
Doing the evening dishes						
By both equally	67	60	71	54	64	79
Mainly by the woman	21	31	13	27	22	14
Mainly by the man	13	9	16	19	14	8
Paying the bills						
By both equally	58	57	58	40	57	73
Mainly by the woman	11	13	9	12	13	8
Mainly by the man	32	30	33	48	30	19
Doing the household cleaning						
By both equally	49	45	52	38	50	57
Mainly by the woman	46	51	42	53	47	40
Mainly by the man	5	3	7	9	4	3
Making the evening meal						
By both equally	47	41	50	40	43	57
Mainly by the woman	45	50	41	49	47	38
Mainly by the man	9	9	9	11	10	5
Doing the washing/ironing						
By both equally	36	33	38	26	36	43
Mainly by the woman	59	61	57	66	58	53
Mainly by the man	5	5	5	7	5	4
Repairing electrical household equipment						
By both equally	33	32	34	22	39	36
Mainly by the woman	6	9	5	12	5	3
Mainly by the man	61	60	61	66	55	62

The opinions expressed revealed that for many household chores young people today feel they should be shared by the man and the woman of the house. Most respondents felt that the effort should be shared on tasks such as deciding what colour to decorate the living room (77 per cent), doing the shopping (68 per cent), doing the evening dishes (67 per cent), and paying the bills (58 per cent). Male respondents (60 per cent) were less keen than female respondents (74 per cent) on the idea of sharing the shopping.

Just under half felt that doing the household cleaning (48 per cent) and still fewer that making the evening meal (36 per cent) should also be shared by the husband and wife. Nearly equal percentages felt, however, that these jobs should be done mainly by the woman.

The one job out of those listed which was seen as the prerogative of the woman was doing the washing and the ironing (by 59 per cent). The one job which should be done mainly by the man was repairing electrical household equipment (60 per cent agreed).

REASONS FOR MARITAL UNHAPPINESS

In a time when, although marriage is not losing popularity, new freedom to leave it once the commitment has been made has increased. As more couples choose the option of divorce or separation, what do young people think about the marriage status? More especially, what do they perceive to be the main cause of marital unhappiness? We gave our youth sample a list of ten possible reasons for marital problems, which were derived from earlier research on interpersonal relationships (Argyle and Henderson 1985). In each case, we asked respondents to say whether they thought that the reason was important or not particularly crucial to marital unhappiness. Table 7.4 shows results for the sample as a whole, and for males and females and different age groups.

Most often nominated as an important factor in the breakdown of happiness was when one partner is unfaithful to another (66 per cent). There were no sex differences, but respondents aged 17 + years (73 per cent) were more likely to say that this was important than 15–16s (63 per cent) or 10–14s (58 per cent). Only two other reasons were endorsed by substantial proportions of respondents and these referred to the failure of marriage partners to share personal feelings (54 per cent) and partners becoming bored with each other (46 per cent). In each of these cases, no differences in extent of endorsement arose

102

Table 7.4 Reasons for marital unhappiness

	All %	Male %	Female %	10–14 %	15–16 %	17 + %
			Sex		Age	
When one partner does not get on well with his or her in-laws						
Don't know	36	37	36	37	37	35
Not so important	54	53	54	50	54	55
Important	10	11	10	12	10	10
When husband and wife do not share household chores						
Don't know	31	29	32	30	28	34
Not so important	61	60	61	62	61	58
Important	9	11	7	7	11	8
When married couples cannot afford a decent home of their own						
Don't know	28	29	27	27	33	26
Not so important	61	58	62	59	59	62
Important	12	13	11	15	8	13
When husband and wife cannot agree on when to start a family						
Don't know	28	26	29	25	30	27
Not so important	60	62	59	62	58	61
Important	13	12	13	13	13	12
When married couples are unable to have children of their own						
Don't know	23	25	22	22	28	20
Not so important	61	59	64	64	57	64
Important	15	16	15	15	15	16
When the husband is against his wife having a job						
Don't know	21	24	20	21	22	21
Not so important	57	58	57	58	58	57
Important	21	19	23	19	22	22
When one partner simply becomes bored with the other						
Don't know	14	10	17	18	13	12
Not so important	40	41	38	46	40	36
Important	46	48	45	36	46	53
When husband is away at work for long periods						
Don't know	13	12	15	16	14	13
Not so important	63	61	65	57	64	67
Important	24	27	20	27	23	21
When husband and wife no longer share personal feelings for each other						
Don't know	11	10	12	18	12	7
Not so important	35	35	35	45	35	28
Important	54	56	52	38	54	65
When one partner is unfaithful to the other						
Don't know	8	6	9	10	10	5
Not so important	26	31	23	32	28	21
Important	66	64	67	58	63	73

between males and females, but notable age differences were evident. Boredom was perceived as important by those aged 17 + (53 per cent) more often than by 15–16s (46 per cent) or 10–14s (36 per cent). Failure to share personal feelings was also perceived to be important more often by respondents aged 17 + years (65 per cent) than by either 15–16s (54 per cent) or 10–14s (38 per cent).

The most trivial or least likely sources of marital problems as perceived by our respondents were lack of sharing household chores (9 per cent) and problems with in-laws (10 per cent). Even when couples could not afford a decent home of their own, that was perceived by relatively few to be an important reason for unhappiness with the marriage relationship.

CONCLUDING REMARKS

Young people exhibited a mixture of broad-mindedness and 'traditional' stereotypes in their beliefs and opinions about the roles of men and women. The nature of the opinion depended a great deal on the particular behaviour or context under consideration.

In the marriage context, for example, most of our respondents were in favour of a sharing of responsibilities of all kinds by husband and wife. If the wife goes out to work, then the husband should share the household chores. Not unexpectedly, females were more likely to favour this arrangement than were males, though even among males a majority supported equality.

Beliefs about the appropriate roles of husband and wife, however, were more complicated than this. When we asked our respondents to consider a range of different domestic chores, there were marked variations across the roles in the extent to which they were allocated either to the husband's or the wife's responsibilities.

Decorating, shopping, washing the dishes, and paying the bills were seen in each case by a majority of respondents to be shared responsibilities. Although, with regard to paying the bills, three times as many respondents felt that this should be done mainly by the husband as by the wife. Very few respondents, however, felt that the household cleaning, cooking the evening meal, or doing the washing/ironing should be done mainly by the man. Cleaning and cooking were thought to be either shared responsibilities or the duties of the wife. Washing and ironing were mostly seen as the wife's responsibility. The one job seen to be principally the husband's duty was repairing electrical household equipment. In summary, although there is evidence that many domestic chores once seen as the responsibility of the woman of the house are now increasingly regarded as duties to be shared by married couples, some traditional stereotyped divisions of responsibility persist among young people.

Moving away from the domestic scene, and turning our attention to women in the world of work, we found that young people are widely in favour of women having equal opportunities with men in the occupational sphere. Women were thought to be suited to work and were better off having their own jobs. Although we did not probe this further, the latter opinion could reflect a feeling not simply that women could be better off financially by working, but that it also makes them better and more fulfilled as people. In general, women were believed to have as much to offer as men at work, to be just as capable of handling important positions in business and industry, and ought not to be restricted in fulfilling any potential they have in those areas by also being married and having a family.

Our sample of young people believed that women should not limit themselves to simply being wives and mothers; they are capable of achieving success, happiness, and fulfilment on both personal and professional fronts, and should be given the freedom and opportunity to do so. There was a feeling, however, that having a family is a serious responsibility in itself and many young people felt that it is wrong for mothers of very small children to go out to work.

As a lead-up to occupational and career development, our respondents tended to believe that women should be encouraged from early on to pursue higher education and professional training for particular jobs. Thus, encouragement should stretch to occupational fields normally thought of as male preserves. Females were markedly more likely than males to agree with these opinions.

On the social scene, too, many traditional stereotypes about appropriate behaviours for women were not widely endorsed by our respondents. Girls should be allowed to stay out late as much as boys, women should be allowed to go or feel comfortable going everywhere a man goes. There was widespread support of going Dutch on dates.

Finally, we investigated opinions about sexual behaviour. Our respondents exhibited broad-minded opinions about sexual relations, although they could not be called promiscuous. Premarital sex was approved of by the great majority, and sex purely for pleasure (rather than just for procreation) was seen by most as acceptable. Many more (though not a majority) were tolerant than were intolerant of sexual relationships other than heterosexual ones. There were mixed feelings about the institution of marriage, although it was interesting that nearly two out of three preferred not to commit themselves either to supporting it or to wanting to see it abolished. On being questioned about causes of marital unhappiness, unfaithfulness, failure to share personal feelings, and partners simply becoming bored with each other were most often identified as important to the breakdown of the relationship.

Chapter Eight

BELIEFS ABOUT RACIAL MINORITIES

Britain, a country that has had in its history English as well as Dutch, French, German, and Scottish monarchs, has had a long history of immigration and emigration. Since the Middle Ages there has been a constant stream of immigrants to Britain, but it is only since the Second World War that immigrant members (from racially distinct groups) have noticeably increased and the topic has become politically controversial.

Walvin has traced the history of migration. He argued:

> The racial attitudes of the British cannot be divorced from the complex history of their imperial adventures. This is not to argue that the British Empire created racial thinking, but rather that the development of racial thinking and imperial advancement were mutually reinforcing and inter-dependent. And, as Empire became ever more important — ever bigger, global and, apparently, vital to Britain's economic and strategic role in the world — it was natural that attitudes should accommodate themselves to that empire. (Walvin 1984: 45)

The 1960s showed the greatest concern with immigration and racial issues. A census in 1966 showed the population to be about 52.5 million, of whom 6 per cent (or about three million) had been born elsewhere. Between the years 1953 and 1957 more people, in fact, left Britain than came to it. At the end of 1965 the total 'non-white' population in the British Isles was estimated at 877,000, of whom 34 per cent were from the Caribbean, 30 per cent from India, 12 per cent from Pakistan, 9 per cent from Africa, 7 per cent from Cyprus, and 8 per cent from elsewhere.

The 1971 census showed that there were just under three million immigrants living in Britain. They are people who are now resident in Britain but were born overseas.

Where do immigrants come from? The biggest single group come from Ireland (703,235), then from Europe (677,295), India and Pakistan (461,930), the West Indies (304,070), Africa (164,205), Australia and New Zealand (78,155), other countries (594,250) (1971 census). Thus, according to the 1971 census, approximately one-third of all immigrants are black — from Asia, Africa, and the West Indies.

In general, more people *leave* Britain to live elsewhere than *come in* as immigrants. For example, during the ten-year period 1968–79 over half a million more people left than entered Britain. In all, 1,993,000 came in and 2,506,500 left, leaving a net loss of 513,500.

The total number of new residents in Britain for 1983 was 202,000 compared to 196,000 in 1973. Of this total the percentage of new residents from the old Commonwealth fell from 25 to 16 per cent while the percentage from Bangladesh, India, and Pakistan rose from 8 to 12 per cent.

Immigrants tend to settle in larger cities where there are jobs, social amenities, and large migrant communities. Hence, the proportion of immigrants in neighbourhoods and cities varies widely. Frequently, the areas where migrants have settled are traditional places such as the inner cities which are themselves frequently associated with decay. But the question of immigrant and race are not exactly the same as Britain or any other country. That is, both immigrants and emigrants may not be of the same racial group as the dominant majority, in the case of Britain, a white Anglo-Celtic-Saxon majority.

The definition of who is black or coloured is a fairly difficult and arbitrary one. In the USA, for example, people of Asian or Indian origin are classified as white. In British government statistics the term 'black' or 'coloured' is usually applied to people who were born in the 'New Commonwealth' and Pakistan or who had one or both parents born there. But the New Commonwealth includes not only people from India, Bangladesh, the West Indies, and Africa but also people from Hong Kong, Singapore, Malta, and Cyprus who would more usually be classified as 'white'.

According to the Office of Population Censuses and Surveys, in 1977 there were an estimated 1.85 million black people (i.e., from the New Commonwealth and Pakistan) living in Britain, i.e., 3.4 per cent of the population. Four out of ten of those people were born in Britain and so are not immigrants at all.

Historically, there has been hostility towards different immigrant groups at different times in British history. In the mid-nineteenth century Irish labourers were frequently discriminated against, attacked, and accused of being immoral and criminal. At the end of the century Jewish immigrants were met with hostility because they were seen to take jobs from the natives. When in the 1950s and 1960s Asian and West Indian immigrants arrived, they tended to take poorly paid and low-status jobs which tended to confirm various existing beliefs about the inferiority of black people. Furthermore, it has been difficult for them to change their status and become upwardly socially mobile.

The topic of race relations and racial attitudes has attracted a great deal of attention, research, and speculation in Britain as well as many other countries. Furthermore, there are sociological and psychological theories, Chester (1976) has suggested two overlapping ways of categorizing theories of racism. The first are victim-system control theories which locate the root or cause of racial injustice either within the environmental control of its primary victims or within the larger social structure. The one end of this victim-system continuum stresses the minority's ability to control, order, or change their circumstances, including attitudes, personality, skills, family, or subculture. The other end of the continuum stresses the external control of the larger social system through authority relations, resource allocations, institutional structures and processes, and cultural norms and symbols. The second are degree of embeddedness theories which suggest either that racism is an isolated and peripheral element of a country's social system or that it is a fundamental root characteristic involved in and perhaps defining the culture's way of life.

Chester set out seven approaches to the causes of racism.

Theories focusing on the characteristics of minorities

These theories may focus on genetic or socio-genic factors and may emphasize a range of factors such as learning difficulties, unwillingness to delay gratification, a subculture of poverty. They focus upon the behaviour of minority groups and individuals and on their ability to control the environment. Then there are theories focusing on personal/ social characteristics of prejudiced persons. These are theories of authoritarianism or ethnocentrism which suggest that for a variety of reasons (inconsistent, neglectful, rejecting child rearing; mental illness; personality deficits) certain people are likely to stress racial differences. They are, it seems, likely to be poorly educated, downwardly mobile, political extremists, from fundamentalist sects. Racism, then, is a response to a social role rather than being a function of minority group membership.

Theories focusing on networks of social relations

These theories examine the naturalness of distinctive groups, contacts between racial groups, and demographic or institutional isolation and segregation. Because racial minorities are not seen to be able to control patterns of group location and interaction, unequal status contacts maintain and advance racism.

Theories focusing on cultural values or ideologies

These theories focus on the systematic value structure of a social system that endorses racism. Societies that advance stratification, segregation, and injustice mean that those discriminated against have no control over their position.

Theories focusing on normal institutional practice or vicious cycles

These approaches suggest that the normal operations of our institutions, historically based on patterns of injustice, serve to perpetuate the vicious cycle of discrimination and injustice. A racist system of cultural values and institutional procedures then sees minority groups developing certain characteristics as a result of prior injustice.

Theories focusing on economic and status self-interest

There are various theories in this predominantly anti-capitalist camp which stress that various élites help confuse non-minority workers about their real interests and consequently serve capitalism's need for economic control and advancement.

Theories focusing on colonialism

These theories all suggest that historical colonial conquest, economic exploitation, political and cultural control as well as a self-

justifying ideology have been the major causes of racism.
Chester concluded thus:

Two general conclusions can be drawn about the state of
theorizing and the relative prominence of the different viewpoints reviewed here. First, there are few theories that are
comprehensive and that encompass the full range of individual
and systemic variables that appear to be involved in American
white racism. The colonial theories come closest to such com-
prehensiveness but, even here, there are few fully developed
perspectives on how the internal colonial paradigm actually
operates. Second, the first two types of theories reviewed seem
to be the most popular, both within the profession and among
the public at large. Much more research and theory has been
developed on minority adaptations and attributes and on white
attitudes than on the other approaches. Both approaches down-
play the roles of group dominance, political and economic conflict and cultural pluralism. In their policy implications, then,
they tend to encourage a focus upon individual and subgroup
changes for minorities and certain whites; this distracts attention from the potential modification of structural characteristics
of our society. Moreover, both types of theories cluster towards
the high end of the victim-system control continuum and
towards the low end of the embeddedness continuum.
    Questions can be raised of why these two types of theories are
so prominent. Are they 'better' theories? Do they explain more?
Is their relative popularity an example of fad and fashion in
social research? Are the theories suited to the kinds of public
views that protect and advance the role of social science? Do
they lead to policies and programs that could advance social
justice concerns? Are they designed (consciously or not) to
support racist myth systems and social structures popular in
the white society? There may be many sociological explanations for their prominence and also for why so many theories
fail to unlock the complex sets of issues involved in white-
controlled and deeply embedded racism. (Chester 1976: 58)

We are concerned with the racial attitudes of young people. Children
as young as four can and do make differential responses to skin colour
and other racial cues, and their racial awareness increases very

quickly after that. However, this does not mean that all children develop negative or antagonistic racial attitudes. Although research has not been able to answer questions like 'Do children who exhibit early awareness develop different attitudes than those who manifest it later?' or 'What is the relationship between earlier expressed preferences and later racism?' it is clear which are some of the major factors that lead to racism. These include:

direct instruction — most prejudice appears to be taught (by parents, schools, the media) rather than caught (from other sources);

reinforcement components — racial attitudes can be punished and rewarded by all sorts of factors which may in turn create or eliminate them;

parental personality — parental personalities often affect their child-rearing techniques and there is evidence that authoritarian parents tend to encourage beliefs and attitudes that are racist;

cognitive factors — people who tend to overcategorize assume that all people from the same category (i.e., racial group) behave in the same way and exhibit the same traits. This cognitive style tends to lead people to be relatively impervious to new information that contradicts their beliefs;

perceptual factors — many children believe that visible differences imply real differences and that the more strange these 'different' people appear the more negative will be people's reaction to them.

Katz (1976) has suggested that the development of racial attitudes is different from that of other attitudes for two major reasons: often information about race comes from people of the same group and there are few models from the out-group to dispel misconceptions; the evaluative (good/bad) component may be more intrinsically involved in early learning with regard to race. Katz also sets out eight steps in the development sequence of racial attitude acquisition:

1. early observation of racial cues;
2. formulation of rudimentary racial concepts;
3. conceptual differentiation between people from different racial groups;
4. recognition that racial characteristics are irrevocable and not subject to change;
5. consolidation of concepts of racial groups;

6. perceptual elaboration between 'us' and 'them';
7. cognitive elaboration;
8. formulation of racial concepts.

Studies done in Britain on race relations and racial attitudes tend to be either socio-historical or empirical. Many writers have speculated on the origin of racial awareness and discrimination in Britain. According to Bloom (1972), recent explanations for the existence of British racism stress five factors: the impermeability of the British class-structure; the homogeneity of British society and culture; the increasing dominance of middle-class values; economic fears; and the psychological vestiges of the stigmata of colonialist pride. Those different factors are not mutually exclusive but different writers have placed more or less emphasis on one or the other. Bloom, however, believes that there are additional factors which need to be taken into account. He lists five:

1. racism and attacks on immigrants have been a substitute for radical social planning and an improvement in the social services;
2. economic instability has aroused long-established working-class fears about unemployment and the cheap labour of immigrants;
3. cultural differences between host and immigrant populations have not decreased nor has understanding increased through poor, clumsy or inept media presentation;
4. 'political leadership has been slow, clumsy, and faltering in combining reassurance, a firm disapproval of racialism, and clear and radical policies to alleviate social and economic distress and uncertainty' (Bloom 1972: 116);
5. legislation has not been used appropriately to eradicate racism.

As well as theoretical explanations for the origin of racism, numerous empirical studies have been done, particularly in schools, to see how multi-racial schools, teachers' attitudes, subject syllabuses affect children's racial beliefs. For instance, Bagley and Verma (1973) devised various measures of racism (i.e., general racism, anti-West Indian, anti-Asian, anti-white) which they gave to 118 white, 58 West Indian, and 44 Asian teenagers aged between 14 and 16 years. They found white teenagers had high general racism scores (half agreed with the idea 'keep Britain white') but that, whereas Asians were fairly

113

anti-West Indian, West Indians had roughly similar scores to Asians on racial issues.

In another study of stereotypes with 281 white English teenagers, Bagley and Verma (1973) noted the positive, neutral, and negative stereotypes of different groups. The Irish were thought to be clean and civilized, but also aggressive, lazy, and untrustworthy. Indians were perceived as civilized, peaceful, and trustworthy but Pakistanis were thought of as untrustworthy, and dirty. Overall, the children seemed to have more positive and less negative stereotypes about West Indians than about Indians who, in turn, were seen more favourably than the Irish and Pakistanis. The negative stereotypes most associated with West Indians were that they were dirty, smelly, aggressive, and unkind; while Indians were thought to be dirty and smelly; the Irish stupid, complaining, troublemakers, aggressive, and drunken; and the Pakistanis dirty and smelly. They conclude:

> Clearly, there is a depressing amount of hostility in the attitudes of white students to their West Indian and Asian class mates. Asian students too have hostile views of other ethnic groups. Only West Indian students have anything approaching an attitudinal set which could be categorized as 'tolerant'. Interestingly, commitment by West Indians to black power ideology is unconnected with hostile perception towards whites. (Bagley and Verma 1973: 258)

Other studies have compared teachers' and pupils' racist and ethnocentric beliefs (Figueroa and Swart 1986) as well as the difference between Asian and English adolescents' perceptions of political institutions (Sharma 1980). However, most of the work in this area appears to be concerned with racism in the schools (Barton 1984).

In our survey we were interested in the attitudes of young people to migrant groups. We chose the three biggest migrant groups: one white, one brown, and one black, partly because they were the largest groups, partly because most research has gone into attitudes towards these three groups and partly because they are the most frequently discussed when considering racial or immigrant issues. The questionnaire items were based on previous research (Ray 1980, 1983, 1984) which has been used in doorstep and postal surveys in Australia, America, Britain, and South Africa. Of course, if one wants to measure racism one must allow respondents to agree or disagree with racist as well as non-racist remarks. There is the possibility, as with all questions on sensitive issues like religion, politics, sex, race, that some questions, by their very nature, give offence but the respondent is always able to disagree with them.

Specifically in our study we were interested in a number of issues:

general racial attitudes such as the extent to which our sample believed they were prejudiced or the extent to which they thought others were the victims of prejudice in Britain. We were particularly interested in their perception of job discrimination and in the perceptions of contact between various racial groups in the country;
minority rights, which were concerned more specifically about whether certain groups should be prevented from various activities and allied to this their reaction to political extremists and to what extent some of their rights should be denied;
attitudes to West Indians;
attitudes to the Irish;
attitudes to Asians;
a comparison of attitudes to these groups on related issues.

GENERAL RACIAL ATTITUDES

We began by asking adolescents how they would describe themselves — as prejudiced against other races or not prejudiced? Asked if they thought of themselves as prejudiced, a disarmingly large number admitted to being either very (10 per cent) or a little (38 per cent) prejudiced, while 42 per cent said that they were not at all prejudiced and 10 per cent did not know. More males (57 per cent) than females (41 per cent) admitted some degree of prejudice and more older (53 per cent) than younger (42 per cent) respondents admitted likewise. It could be argued either that these respondents are being particularly honest as fewer adults admit prejudice or that a certain amount of bravado is associated with racial prejudice and that this tended to over-inflate scores.

We asked identical questions about the racial prejudice experienced by Asians (Indians and Pakistanis) and Blacks (Africans and West Indians) but found almost identical responses. In all, 42 per cent thought the above groups suffered a lot of prejudice in Britain nowadays, 32 per cent a little prejudice and between 8 and 11 per cent hardly any. Between 15 and 18 per cent did not know and there were no sex or class differences. In all, therefore, nearly three-quarters of our sample believed that racial minorities experienced some racial prejudice. Interestingly, more older (83 per cent) than younger (63 per cent) children thought that prejudice occurred to these racially identifiable minority groups.

We then asked 'Do you think that the majority of coloured people in between are superior or inferior or equal to you?' On the issue of racial equality 60 per cent agreed that coloured people were equal to them, though more females than males agreed (65 per cent vs. 55 per cent) and more older than younger adolescent respondents (66 per cent vs. 51 per cent). Roughly the same number (18 per cent) as 'did not know' thought 'coloured' peoples inferior (17 per cent) and a small minority (2–8 per cent) thought them superior. There were no sex, age, and class differences.

We asked our sample whether they thought Asian and black Britons suffered job discrimination and again the results were so similar that it could be argued that respondents saw no difference in job discrimination against these two groups. About a third (30–4 per cent) thought racial job discrimination happened a lot and 45 per cent that it sometimes occurred and 10–12 per cent said it rarely happened, thus indicating that, overall, three-quarters thought that it is a non-rare occurrence. On this issue there were no sex, age, or class differences.

We also asked the adolescents' attitudes to racial discrimination legislation. About half (48 per cent) were in favour and just under a third (30 per cent) 'did not know' but a fifth (22 per cent) opposed it. Females more than males (52 per cent vs. 45 per cent) and older more than younger children (57 per cent vs. 39 per cent) were in favour of this sort of legislation. Naturally there was a higher incidence of 'don't know' among the younger children.

Finally, we attempted to measure the social distance concept which relates to contact with other races. There were completely consistent sex, and to a lesser extent, age differences on the five questions that we asked. Although nearly half (47 per cent) said they would mind a little or a lot if a relative married a person of Asian origin, only a third (36 per cent) said they would mind (a little or a lot) if a close relative married a person of black or Irish origin. If we had separated out the three groups (Asian, Irish, West Indian), however, as was done later in the questionnaire, it is quite possible that the respondents would have shown different patterns of prejudices to these different ethnic groups.

Two out of three (64 per cent) adolescents said they would not try to avoid having neighbours from the West Indies, India, and Pakistan. On the issue of whether local authorities or private landlords should refuse accommodation to West Indians, Indians, or Pakistanis just over half (54 per cent) believed that accommodation should be let to these groups and about one in four said they did not know (26 per cent). One in five (21 per cent) believed that these three groups should not be given accommodation.

In every instance, females reported less prejudice than males, and the older respondents seemed less prejudiced than younger respondents who nearly always had a much bigger 'don't know' score. While roughly two-thirds of the sample either expressed no desire to avoid contact with other groups or did not express an opinion, between a fifth and a third of the respondents clearly would prefer to avoid any sort of contact with members from other groups.

RIGHTS OF GROUPS WITH MINORITY BELIEFS

We were interested in two issues in this section. The first was the extent to which people with overtly racist views (people who say that all black and Asian people should be forced to leave Britain) should be allowed or prevented from expressing those views to different types of audience. Second, we were particularly interested in the extent to which subjects discriminated between the rights of racists vs. revolutionaries (people who wish to overturn the government of Britain) to propagate their beliefs.

Nearly two in three of the respondents believed that people with overtly racial views should be allowed to hold public meetings (64 per cent) and publish books (63 per cent) expressing their views. Twenty-three per cent were against both of these things. Just under half thought that these minorities should be allowed to teach in schools (47 per cent) or teach in colleges or universities (48 per cent). Between 10 and 15 per cent said they did not know. Older adolescents tended to be more liberal than younger children, particularly with respect to public meetings and publishing books, but less liberal about allowing racists to teach in schools.

When the same four questions were asked about revolutionaries who wished to overthrow the British government by revolution a similar pattern resulted but the respondents were overall less sympathetic to them. Whereas just over half (53 per cent) thought they should be allowed to publish books, under half (49 per cent) thought they should be allowed to hold public meetings. But less than a third approved of revolutionaries teaching in schools or universities. Females and younger respondents tended to have fewer 'don't know' scores and lower 'no' scores than males and older respondents who seemed less tolerant of revolutionaries.

Taken together, these results seem to indicate that young people find the expression of racial views more acceptable than that of the views of revolutionaries though they appear not to relish hearing either of these views at school, and for the most part they were undecided about the expression of views in colleges and universities.

ATTITUDES TO WEST INDIANS

We asked our respondents to indicate the extent to which they agreed or disagreed with fifteen statements about people of West Indian extraction living in Britain. The two statements that revealed highest consensus were both positive and non-discriminatory. About two-thirds of the sample believed that West Indians were just as good at doing clerical work and just as hard-working as native white Britons. But females did agree more than males and older children more than younger children on both these items.

Just over half thought West Indians had been unfairly discriminated against (55 per cent), disagreed that they should be separated from other groups (57 per cent), and that because of poorer educational opportunities they found it harder to get a job (53 per cent). Once again females tended to be non-discriminatory and more liberal than males but whereas older respondents tended to agree more with the first item they tended to agree less with the latter two items.

Fewer than one in five of the sample agreed with the negative items that the granting of educational opportunities to West Indians is a dangerous thing, and that drunkenness is a major problem with West Indians. Again in both cases males more than females and younger more than older children tended to agree with this.

Almost exactly half the sample believed that West Indians deserve better than they get in this country and disagreed that West Indians did not show much inclination to work. Once again females showed themselves to be more tolerant than males by agreeing more with

Table 8.1 Attitudes to West Indians

		All %	Sex Male %	Sex Female %	Age 10–14 %	Age 15–16 %	Age 17 + %
1. West Indians deserve better than they get in this country at the moment	Agree Neither Disagree	50 24 26	44 22 34	54 26 20	56 24 20	49 23 28	42 26 32
2. The West Indians should be kept as separate as possible from other races	Agree Neither Disagree	22 21 57	27 21 52	19 21 60	30 21 49	25 20 55	15 21 64
3. The granting of wide educational opportunities to the West Indians is a dangerous thing	Agree Neither Disagree	19 33 48	22 33 45	17 34 49	21 39 40	20 33 47	17 27 56
4. Many West Indians are just as good at doing clerical work as white people	Agree Neither Disagree	68 17 15	64 18 18	74 17 9	69 17 14	67 16 17	71 16 13
5. West Indians generally don't show much inclination to work	Agree Neither Disagree	24 27 49	29 44 27	32 52 16	25 30 45	22 29 49	14 31 55
6. West Indians are kind and gentle people	Agree Neither Disagree	31 47 22	27 26 47	19 28 53	36 44 20	29 44 27	30 51 19
7. West Indians have been unfairly discriminated against	Agree Neither Disagree	55 28 17	51 27 22	57 28 15	54 31 15	52 28 20	58 24 18
8. Drunkenness is one of the greatest problems with West Indians	Agree Neither Disagree	15 42 43	18 39 43	12 45 43	21 36 43	17 40 43	8 45 47
9. West Indians are generally not very hygiene conscious	Agree Neither Disagree	29 35 36	31 33 36	27 37 36	30 38 32	31 32 37	25 34 41
10. West Indians often get into fights with one another	Agree Neither Disagree	25 42 33	28 39 33	24 46 30	31 41 28	26 41 33	21 46 33
11. Given the chance, West Indians will work as hard as white people	Agree Neither Disagree	67 19 14	62 20 18	73 19 8	64 20 16	67 18 15	69 19 12
12. It is only because they haven't had the same chance to get an education that West Indians find it harder to get work	Agree Neither Disagree	53 25 23	51 23 26	55 26 19	57 25 18	51 26 23	50 23 27

Table 8.1 (cont.)

			All %	Sex Male %	Female %	Age 10–14 %	15–16 %	17 + %
13.	The West Indians are a rather ugly race	Agree	27	31	23	30	28	23
		Neither	30	30	30	32	27	30
		Disagree	43	39	47	38	45	47
14.	We could learn a lot from the way West Indians share with one another everything they've got	Agree	44	42	46	41	41	45
		Neither	35	34	37	36	37	34
		Disagree	21	24	17	23	22	21
15.	Generally West Indians are more musical than whites	Agree	36	36	37	37	32	41
		Neither	38	34	42	39	38	37
		Disagree	26	30	21	24	30	22

the former item and disagreeing less with the latter item.

The majority response was neither to agree nor disagree on some items such as the West Indians are kind and gentle, more musical, and rather bellicose. Some rather negative stereotypes were rejected by more subjects than accepted them, such as that West Indians are generally not very hygiene conscious and rather ugly as a race. Certainly the overall results suggested that the adolescents agreed more with positive items and disagreed more with negative items, though a fairly large number remained uncommitted.

ATTITUDES TO THE IRISH

The Irish were seen by the majority to be good at clerical work and as hard-working as others and there was 50 per cent disagreement with the idea that they do not show much inclination to work. Nearly half actually disagreed with various negative stereotypes — i.e., that the Irish are not very hygiene conscious and rather ugly but almost twice as many agreed as disagreed that drunkenness is a problem with the Irish and that they often get into fights with one another.

Some of the items yielded very high neither, agree nor disagree scores, such as the fact that the Irish are kind and gentle, more musical than other people, or that we could learn a lot from the way they share with one another. Many of the items showed a sex difference and there was a highly consistent pattern — females tended to agree more and disagree less than males with 'positive' items that claimed the Irish to be as good as natives or even having special qualities, but

Table 8.2 Attitudes to the Irish

			All %	Sex Male %	Female %	10–14 %	Age 15–16 %	17 + %
1.	The Irish deserve better than they get in this country	Agree	43	42	44	47	45	37
		Neither	36	35	38	33	35	41
		Disagree	21	23	18	20	20	22
2.	Many Irish people are just as good at doing clerical work as other people	Agree	70	66	74	68	72	72
		Neither	20	21	17	21	18	20
		Disagree	10	13	9	11	10	8
3.	The Irish generally don't show much inclination to work	Agree	21	23	18	25	22	14
		Neither	29	28	30	31	28	27
		Disagree	50	49	52	44	50	59
4.	Irish people are kind and gentle people	Agree	39	39	40	38	39	41
		Neither	43	40	46	41	44	45
		Disagree	18	22	14	21	17	14
5.	Irish people have been unfairly discriminated against	Agree	45	41	48	46	45	43
		Neither	33	33	33	34	32	33
		Disagree	22	26	19	20	23	24
6.	Drunkenness is one of the greatest problems with Irish people	Agree	40	44	36	44	35	42
		Neither	35	32	38	34	37	34
		Disagree	25	24	26	22	28	24
7.	The Irish are generally not very hygiene conscious	Agree	18	21	14	24	17	12
		Neither	37	37	36	38	35	36
		Disagree	45	42	50	38	48	52
8.	The Irish often get into fights with one another	Agree	42	46	37	44	37	43
		Neither	35	31	40	34	36	35
		Disagree	23	23	23	22	27	22
9.	Given the chance, the Irish will work as hard as other people	Agree	69	67	72	62	71	74
		Neither	21	20	21	25	19	18
		Disagree	10	13	7	13	10	8
10.	It is only because they haven't had the same chance to get an education that the Irish find it harder to get work	Agree	32	30	33	39	31	25
		Neither	38	37	41	36	39	41
		Disagree	30	33	26	25	30	34
11.	The Irish are a rather ugly race	Agree	19	21	16	26	17	13
		Neither	33	34	32	34	30	34
		Disagree	48	45	52	40	53	53
12.	We could learn a lot from the way the Irish share with one another everything they've got	Agree	26	26	26	26	29	23
		Neither	50	50	51	46	50	54
		Disagree	24	24	23	28	21	23
13.	Generally Irish people are more musical than other people	Agree	21	21	21	24	20	19
		Neither	48	44	52	44	49	50
		Disagree	31	35	27	32	31	31

Table 8.3 Attitudes to Asians

				Sex		Age	
		All %	Male %	Female %	10–14 %	15–16 %	17+ %
1.	Asian people have been	Agree	56	54	58	58	57	55
	unfairly discriminated	Neither	24	23	28	19	24	23
	against	Disagree	20	23	14	23	19	22
2.	Asian people generally	Agree	28	32	23	31	29	34
	don't show much	Neither	33	30	37	36	33	30
	inclination to work	Disagree	39	38	40	33	38	36
3.	The granting of wide	Agree	21	23	18	26	21	16
	educational opportunities	Neither	40	39	42	40	41	48
	to Asians is a dangerous	Disagree	39	38	40	33	38	36
	thing							
4.	The Asians should be	Agree	25	29	21	27	27	20
	kept as separate as	Neither	24	24	25	28	21	24
	possible from other races	Disagree	51	47	54	45	52	56
5.	Drunkenness is one of	Agree	14	16	13	19	16	8
	the greatest problems	Neither	40	38	43	38	40	42
	with Asians	Disagree	46	46	44	43	44	50
6.	Asians often get into	Agree	23	25	20	28	20	20
	fights with one another	Neither	43	39	47	41	44	43
		Disagree	34	36	33	31	36	37
7.	The Asians are a rather	Agree	29	35	23	30	29	27
	ugly race	Neither	33	31	35	38	31	30
		Disagree	38	34	42	32	40	43
8.	Generally, Asians are	Agree	16	18	14	19	15	13
	more musical than	Neither	48	43	52	48	47	47
	whites	Disagree	36	39	34	33	38	40
9.	We could learn a lot from	Agree	28	30	27	31	25	27
	the way Asian people	Neither	44	41	49	43	45	45
	share with one another	Disagree	28	29	24	26	30	28
	everything they've got							
10.	Given the chance,	Agree	57	53	62	55	56	60
	Asians will work as	Neither	26	26	26	29	25	24
	hard as white people	Disagree	17	21	12	16	19	16
11.	Asian people deserve	Agree	45	40	50	46	45	44
	better than they get in	Neither	30	30	31	33	29	28
	this country at the	Disagree	25	30	19	21	26	28
	moment							
12.	Many Asian people are	Agree	54	50	59	54	54	56
	just as good at doing	Neither	29	30	27	33	26	27
	clerical work as white	Disagree	17	20	14	13	20	17
	people							
13.	It is only because they	Agree	41	39	43	43	39	40
	haven't had the same	Neither	33	31	36	28	31	31
	chance to get an educa-	Disagree	26	30	21	29	30	29
	tion that Asians find it							
	harder to get work							

there was the very opposite pattern for negative items.

There were fewer age differences but when they were significant they showed that older subjects tended to be more like the females when compared to males — that is more positive and less negative than younger subjects.

ATTITUDES TO ASIANS

We asked the same thirteen questions about Asians as we did about West Indians and a similar pattern arose. First, there was in general more agreement than disagreement about positive items especially the idea that Asians will work as hard as whites, have been unfairly discriminated against, and deserve better than they get. Also there was general disagreement about negative items especially that they should be kept as separate as possible, or that Asians are lazy, drunken, or bellicose. There were also fairly high don't know answers.

Furthermore, the same sex and age pattern emerged. More females than males were more positive and less negative to Asians, and where significant age differences occurred generally older respondents were more positive and less negative than younger respondents.

COMPARING ATTITUDES TO THE THREE GROUPS

In order to compare the racial attitudes of our respondents to the three major immigrant groups, we grouped the eight positive and seven negative statements that made up our questionnaire. The positive statements showed an interesting pattern. Whereas half the sample believed West Indians deserve better than they get in this country, only 43 per cent believed this true of the Irish. Curiously, fewer thought Asians as good at doing clerical work as West Indians and the Irish although a much larger number had no opinion.

The Irish were thought to be kind and gentle by more than thought West Indians and Asians kind and gentle but fewer expressed an agree or disagree opinion than gave either. Almost equal numbers (55 per cent vs. 56 per cent) thought West Indians and Asians had been unfairly discriminated against, but 10 per cent fewer that the Irish have experienced a similar fate (45 per cent). However, one in three expressed no opinion about discrimination against the Irish.

Over two in three believed the West Indians and Irish worked as hard as native Britons but curiously only 57 per cent thought this true

Table 8.4 Racial attitudes to Asians, West Indians, and Irish in this country

	Agree %	Neither %	Disagree %
Positive Statements:			
1. a) *West Indians* deserve better than they get in this country	50	24	26
b) *Asians* deserve better than they get in this country	45	30	25
c) The *Irish* deserve better than they get in this country	43	36	21
2. a) Many *West Indians* are just as good at doing clerical work as white people	68	17	15
b) Many *Asians* are just as good at doing clerical work as white people	54	29	17
c) Many *Irish* people are just as good at doing clerical work as white people	70	20	10
3. a) *West Indians* are kind and gentle people	31	47	22
b) *Asians* are kind and gentle people	32	46	22
c) The *Irish* are kind and gentle people	39	43	18
4. a) *West Indians* have been unfairly discriminated against	55	28	17
b) *Asians* have been unfairly discriminated against	56	24	20
c) The *Irish* have been unfairly discriminated against	45	33	22
5. a) Given the chance, *West Indians* will work as hard as white people	67	19	14
b) Given the chance, *Asians* will work as hard as white people	57	26	17
c) Given the chance, the *Irish* will work as hard as white people	69	21	10
6. a) It is only because they haven't had the same chance to get an education that *West Indians* find it harder to get work	53	25	22
b) It is only because they haven't had the same chance to get an education that *Asians* find it harder to get work	41	33	26
c) It is only because they haven't had the same chance to get an education that the *Irish* find it harder to get work	32	38	30
7. a) We could learn a lot from the way *West Indians* share with one another everything they've got	44	35	21
b) We could learn a lot from the way *Asians* share with one another everything they've got	28	46	26
c) We could learn a lot from the way the *Irish* share with one another everything they've got	26	50	24
8. a) Generally, *West Indians* are more musical than white people	36	38	26
b) Generally, *Asians* are more musical than white people	16	48	36
c) Generally, the *Irish* are more musical than white people	21	48	31

Table 8.5 Racial attitudes to Asians, West Indians, and Irish in this country

	Agree %	Neither %	Disagree %
Negative Statements:			
1. a) *West Indians* generally don't show much inclination to work	24	27	49
b) *Asians* generally don't show much inclination to work	28	33	39
c) The *Irish* generally don't show much inclination to work	21	29	50
2. a) Drunkenness is one of the great problems with *West Indians*	15	42	43
b) Drunkenness is one of the great problems with *Asians*	14	40	46
c) Drunkenness is one of the great problems with the *Irish*	40	35	25
3. a) *West Indians* are generally not hygiene conscious	29	35	36
b) *Asians* are generally not hygiene conscious	20	48	32
c) The *Irish* are generally not hygiene conscious	18	37	45
4. a) *West Indians* often get into fights with one another	25	42	33
b) *Asians* often get into fights with one another	23	43	34
c) The *Irish* often get into fights with one another	43	34	23
5. a) *West Indians* are a rather ugly race	42	35	23
b) *Asians* are a rather ugly race	29	33	38
c) The *Irish* are a rather ugly race	19	33	48
6. a) *West Indians* should be kept as separate as possible from other races	22	21	57
b) *Asians* should be kept as separate as possible from other races	25	24	51
7. a) The granting of wider educational opportunities to the *West Indians* is a dangerous thing	19	33	48
b) The granting of wider educational opportunities to the *Asians* is a dangerous thing	21	36	43

of Asians. This is a particularly surprising finding given the stereotype often associated with people from India and Pakistan, namely that they are extremely industrious.

The final three questions all showed more agreement when it came to West Indians than the other two groups. West Indians were perceived to have more educational disadvantages, a better record of sharing, and to be more musical than the other groups. Another consistent pattern was the number of people who neither agreed nor disagreed with questions about the Irish, though the reason for this is not clear.

The seven negative questions showed by and large higher disagreement than agreement scores for all three groups though some common stereotypes were reaffirmed. For instance over 40 per cent thought drunkenness a problem associated with the Irish and that they frequently get into fights with one another. West Indians were thought of by more (though less than a third) to be less hygiene conscious than the other groups and far fewer disagreed with the statement that they are a rather ugly race. Interestingly, whereas about half (48 per cent) disagreed that the granting of wider educational opportunities to West Indians is a dangerous thing, only a third (33 per cent) disagreed with the same statement when applied to Asians possibly because the latter are seen as more of a threat.

CONCLUDING REMARKS

Questions about racial discrimination and prejudice frequently engender passions. For some it is even immoral to 'measure' racial prejudice because this often involves the possibility of allowing the expression of negative or discriminatory statements. Nevertheless, it is an important issue in any nation that has a number of identifiable ethnic groups and it warrants periodic investigation.

For some, these results should bring hope. There was evidence of racial prejudice and discrimination, indeed over a third admitted that they were 'a little' prejudiced, but the vast majority who expressed opinions believed in equality between 'races', the use of anti-discriminatory legislation, close integration between groups. The majority did not oppose the view that explicit racial attitudes be banned. There was some evidence that stereotypes were confirmed — the Irish as drunken and bellicose, the West Indians as musical — but fewer than half the sample endorsed these stereotypes. Moreover, some stereotypes were disconfirmed — that Asians are hard working, for instance.

Three consistent findings occurred. Females nearly always express less negative racial prejudice than males. That is, they were more in favour of equality, endorsed fewer negative statements, and agreed with more positive statements than the males. This is consistent with previous findings on sex differences (see chapter 2) though it is not always clear why it arises.

There were also a fairly large number of age differences which were usually linear, though there were a number of inconsistencies. Older respondents tended to be more 'liberal' in their responses. For instance, they believed that more discrimination occurred, were more against the silencing of publicly expressed racist views but tended to reject stereotypes and negative statements and accept positive statements more often than did younger children. A number of reasons could be put forward for these findings — such as the fact that older adolescents are more aware of racial issues in society; more sympathetic to the plight of others and less egocentric; or quite simply more aware of the socially desirable responses that could be given. Each of the above, or indeed other explanations, could be put forward for these findings.

Finally, between one in four and one in three of the sample, on average, chose the mid-point of the five- or three-point response scale — in other words gave no opinion. As always, it is difficult to explain this response. It may result from the fact that some people in the sample — from Northern Ireland or rural parts of Scotland — had no or little experience of ethnic groups or it may be that respondents preferred not to classify whole groups, believing statements to be true of some members of the group, untrue of others and thus, for the group as a whole, the mid-point was the obvious answer. Some may have preferred not to answer these questions on such a sensitive topic. But, as there were over 2,000 adolescents in the sample, enough non-mid-point responses were obtained to give a good idea about their attitudes to race.

Finally, as was pointed out in the introduction, attitudes and behaviour are far from positively correlated. Hence those expressing negative and discriminatory attitudes may not act as such or vice versa. However, on the basis of these findings, it is possible to conclude that the majority of young native Britons are sympathetic to the difficulties of ethnic groups and, for the most part, relatively free of prejudice.

Chapter Nine

RELIGION AND THE PARANORMAL

A number of social surveys have indicated that, on the basis of both attitudinal and behavioural measures, the significance of religion for people in Britain has been on the decline over the past twenty years. Recorded adult membership of the larger religious denominations declined between 1975 and 1985. Meanwhile, there has been some growth among small, independent, and non-Christian religions. Membership of non-Christian groups, for example, increased from around 800,000 in 1975 to over a million in 1980, owing mainly to a 50 per cent increase in the number of Muslims. There were significant increases, too, in the number of Hindus and Sikhs over the same five-year period (Ramprakash 1986).

While a majority of people in this country seem to have attended church or a religious service at some time, only a minority claim to be regular church-goers. Heald and Wybrow (1986) reported that 20 per cent of the general public said that they attended religious services at least once a month. Around one in four said that they went a few times a year or almost never (23 per cent each), while one in three (34 per cent) never attended religious services.

Among people who considered themselves to be very religious — numbering some 8 per cent of the general public — 61 per cent said they attended religious services almost every week or more often. Three out of four regular church-goers (at least once a month) said that they had attended religious services at least that often five years ago, while one in five said they had not.

Some people attend church for special occasions as well as or rather than as a matter of routine. Heald and Wybrow reported that around one in ten (8 per cent) of the public surveyed by Gallup said that they attended religious services at Christmas or Easter only. Twelve per cent attended on special occasions as much as once a year, while

8 per cent did so less often. Almost one in two (47 per cent) said that they never went to religious services. The latter tended to be males (59 per cent) and the under-30s (56 per cent).

Whether or not they attended religious services, many people nevertheless thought of themselves as religious or as believing in God. Heald and Wybrow found a gender gap in how religious people felt they were. Forty per cent of men said they were not religious at all compared with 29 per cent of women. More older people than younger people rated themselves as very religious. Among the 16–24s, however, just 2 per cent rated themselves as very religious, 42 per cent as somewhat religious, and 52 per cent as not religious at all. Despite lack of atttendance, 70 per cent said they believed in God and one in three (31 per cent) believed in the Devil.

Religious belief has changed in prevalence over time, however, and varies a good deal with age. Younger people tend to believe less than do older people. The surveys by Gallup revealed that 57 per cent of 16–19s believed in God compared with 75 per cent of over 65s. Among the younger ones, 33 per cent believed in a life after death compared with 45 per cent of elderly people. Young adults are less likely to hold a whole range of religious beliefs than are elderly people. There are some interesting exceptions though. The under-20s are more likely than older people to believe in astrological predictions (Heald and Wybrow 1986).

Surveys of religious belief have indicated a decline in religious commitment in recent years. Haldane (1978), for instance, reported that 58 per cent of a national sample claimed to be 'very' or 'fairly' religious in 1968 compared with 49 per cent of a London-only sample in 1978. In 1968, 50 per cent said they were certain there is a God; in 1978 42 per cent agreed with this. The 1978 survey revealed that marginally more women than men fell into the group to whom religion is an important element in their lives. There was a marked increase in religious belief with age and a considerable difference between social classes, with the working classes much higher than middle classes. Although the samples in these two surveys are not precisely comparable, the same questions and statements were used and they do serve to provide some general indication of trends in religious belief.

In our youth survey, we were interested in finding out about the religious activities and beliefs of young people in Britain today. We asked questions about regularity of church attendance, both for special occasions and as a matter of weekly routine. We were also interested in belief in God, strength of religious feeling, and related behaviour such as prayer. In addition to traditional religiosity, however, we also asked about fringe beliefs connected with astrology, spiritualism, and paranormal phenomena.

RELIGIOSITY AND AFFILIATION

Most of our respondents (61 per cent) claimed to have a religion, while just over one in four (28 per cent) said they did not. On the other hand, these figures were reversed when they were asked whether they belonged to or attended a local religious organization or a church. Twenty-eight per cent said that they did, while 61 per cent said that they did not.

CHURCH ATTENDANCE ON SPECIAL OCCASIONS

One measure of having some connection with religion is attendance at church. People may go to church for all kinds of reasons, however, and mere physical appearance inside a church does not necessarily mean that a person holds religious beliefs. Church attendance for special occasions may be more for social events than for religious ones. Among the youth sample interviewed in this study, only a minority (12 per cent) had been to a religious service during the year to mark a special occasion such as a wedding, funeral, or festival. Around one in three (35 per cent) said they had not been at all, while more than half (54 per cent) did not know for sure whether they had or not. The youngest respondents, aged 10–14 (19 per cent), were more likely than the older ones (9 per cent) to have attended church. Among those who indicated that they had attended some special religious service, the largest proportion (43 per cent) had done so just once or twice in the past year. Nearly one in five (17 per cent) said they had never attended despite the fact they had indicated that they had on the previous question. The 10–14s (19 per cent) were more likely than 15 + s (7 per cent) to have been five times or more. It seems likely, therefore, that among a minority of young people there is considerable uncertainty about church attendance. Among those who claimed they had attended religious services in the last year, for many this was a funeral (44 per cent). For around one in four (25 per cent) it was either a wedding or a funeral.

ROUTINE CHURCH ATTENDANCE

Attendance at occasional religious services for festivals, weddings, or funerals may signify little about religiosity. Routine church attendance, however, is probably more likely to occur among those who have a religious affiliation or conviction. Outside special occasions, only a small minority (12 per cent) of young people had been to a regular or normal religious service in the last year. Most (60 per cent) said they had not, and 29 per cent did not know. Males (15 per cent) attended services more often than females (9 per cent) and 10–14s (19 per cent) more often than either 15–16s (12 per cent) or 17 + s (5 per cent).

Of those who volunteered that they had been to a regular religious service, one in three (33 per cent) had attended at least once a week. Somewhat more (39 per cent) had attended less often, while nearly one in three (30 per cent) were uncertain. The 10–14s (48 per cent) were more likely than 15–16s (35 per cent) or more especially the 17 + s (18 per cent) to attend once a week or more.

IMPORTANCE OF THE CHURCH AND RELIGION

Regardless of whether or not individuals go to church or some other place of worship regularly, how important do they think it is to do so? And how important is religion in the lives of young people? On the first question, one in three (34 per cent) felt that it is important actually to go to a place of worship regularly. These were outnumbered by young people (45 per cent) who did not endorse this sentiment. More than six out of ten youth respondents (62 per cent) said that religion was important to them, entirely outnumbering those who said that it was not important to them (39 per cent). When asked to identify the more important things about religion, teaching a good life was the aim most often endorsed (by 45 per cent), followed by believing in God (29 per cent), and then going to a place of worship (23 per cent). All these questions yielded similar age differences (see table 9.1).

PRAYER

Another behaviour associated with religious affiliation and belief is prayer. Only a minority of youth respondents (14 per cent) said that they prayed. More than two and a half times as many (37 per cent) said that they never prayed, even in times of crisis. The youngest, 10–14s (20 per cent), claimed to pray more often than the oldest, 17 + (7 per cent), with the 15–16-year-olds (15 per cent) falling behind the two. Among those who said that they did pray, many (43 per cent) did so several times a day, 17 per cent once a day, and 8 per cent only during times of stress or crisis. Among those who prayed, females (48 per cent) were more likely to pray several times a day than were males (37 per cent).

BELIEF IN GOD OR A SUPERNATURAL BEING

While the belief that life's events are influenced by the stars may be widespread, this does not preclude the belief that life is predetermined in some way by some higher force — whether this is God or some other supernatural being. Around one in four of this youth sample (26 per cent) said that they believed in the existence of a higher force which has some influence over events in their lives. Somewhat more (36 per cent) dismissed this belief, while marginally more again (39 per cent) were uncertain. The youngest respondents, 10–14 years (40 per cent), were far more likely to believe in a higher force than either 15–16s (26 per cent) or 17 + s (15 per cent).

On the question of the existence of God, fewer than one in five (17 per cent) said that they thought about it from time to time, 94 per cent said they did not, while more than half (55 per cent) were unsure about this. Regardless of whether they gave the matter any thought, equal proportions of young people (28 per cent) either believed or did not believe in God. Many (45 per cent) did not know, however.

Table 9.1 Importance of the church and religion

		Sex			Age	
	All	Male	Female	10–14	15–16	17 +
	%	%	%	%	%	%
What is your opinion about attending a church or place of worship regularly? Is it an important thing that you ought to do or not?						
Yes	34	32	36	45	33	26
No	45	47	43	37	44	52
Don't know	21	21	21	18	23	23
Regardless of whether you go to a church or place of worship or not, how important is religion in your life?						
Very important	31	32	30	26	36	30
Fairly important	30	29	31	36	27	29
Not very important	24	20	28	27	25	23
Not important	15	19	11	11	13	18
People disagree over religion: they can even disagree about what religion is: what do you think are the most important things about religion?						
Going to a place of worship	22	21	24	28	22	19
Believing in God	29	27	30	45	44	46
Leading a good life	44	46	43	45	44	46
Don't know	5	6	4	9	3	3

BELIEF IN AN AFTER-LIFE AND HEAVENLY WORLD

Does all life end after death, or is there an after-life? If there is an after-life, is it spent in heaven or in hell, depending presumably on how many merit or demerit points picked up during life?

A little over one in four (25 per cent) of young people said they had thought about whether there is a life after death. Half as many again (18 per cent) did not believe they ever had, even at moments of crisis. Most (70 per cent), however, did not know. The youngest respondents, aged 10–14 years (19 per cent), were more likely than either the 15–16s (12 per cent) or 17 + s (5 per cent) to say they had ever thought about an after-life. Despite the apparent lack of enthusiasm for thinking about the idea, one in three (33 per cent) admitted to a belief in life after death, outnumbering those (24 per cent) who did not believe. Forty-four per cent did not know. Once again the youngest — 10–14s — were more likely (43 per cent) than the older ones (29 per cent) to say they believed in life after death. A similar proportion (32 per cent) also believed in heaven and hell, though rather more (30 per cent) on this occasion held doubts. Males (34 per cent) were more likely to have doubts about heaven and hell than were females (25 per cent).

ASTROLOGY AND SUPERSTITION

In addition to opinions about religious convictions, the survey also asked youth about beliefs in other spiritual and psychical phenomena which exist on the fringes of religion. A lot of people today read the astrology columns in newspapers and magazines and follow the predictions under their own signs. To what extent do young people do this, and how much of what they read do they believe?

Few (11 per cent) had ever had their fortunes told; most never had (69 per cent). Even fewer (6 per cent) admitted ever looking at what their stars say in newspapers and magazines; but a large majority (81 per cent) were unable to say for sure whether they did or not. Males (20 per cent) were much more certain than females (6 per cent) that they did not follow their star sign predictions.

Among those who said that they did read their stars, those who believed (28 per cent) were outnumbered by those who did not believe what astrological predictions had to say (37 per cent). The remainder (33 per cent) were uncertain one way or the other. Around half

Table 9.2 Astrology and superstition

| | | Sex | | | Age | |
	All %	Male %	Female %	10–14 %	15–16 %	17 + %
Has your future ever been told?						
Yes	11	12	9	18	12	23
No	69	66	71	66	62	71
Don't know	20	22	20	16	26	6
Do you ever look at what your stars say in the newspapers or magazines?						
Yes	6	7	4	10	7	1
No	13	20	6	12	11	15
Don't know	81	73	90	79	83	83
If yes:						
Do you believe in what it says?						
Yes	29	28	29	35	25	25
No	37	44	32	33	35	48
Don't know	34	27	39	32	41	28
Would you describe yourself, in general, as a superstitious person?						
Yes	18	19	16	26	16	12
No	49	55	42	43	44	55
Don't know	33	27	43	31	40	34

(49 per cent) said they would not describe themselves as superstitious; just under one in five (18 per cent) said that they would. As can be seen in table 9.2, the respondents admitted progressively to less superstition as they grow older.

BELIEF IN GHOSTS

Despite the popularity since the end of the 1970s, especially with young audiences, of horror movies with story-lines in which paranormal phenomena are central factors, thinking about or belief in ghosts was not widespread. Fewer than one in ten (8 per cent) said they ever thought about things such as ghosts, and under one in five (19 per cent) said they believed in such things. There was widespread uncertainty on both counts, with males being more often certain than were females that they doubted the existence of ghosts and related phenomena. Among the minority who did think there are ghosts, one in five (20 per cent) said they had had personal experience of such

Table 9.3 Belief in ghosts

	All %	Sex Male %	Female %	10-14 %	Age 15-16 %	17 + %
Have you ever thought about such things (as ghosts)?						
Yes	8	9	7	11	11	2
No	12	14	9	12	12	10
Don't know	81	77	85	78	77	88
Do you believe that there are such things as ghosts or poltergeists, or anything like that, or not?						
Yes	19	17	20	21	19	17
No	24	28	19	20	23	25
Don't know	58	55	61	59	58	58
If yes:						
Why do you think there are ghosts?						
Personal experience	20	17	21	29	21	9
The reports of people I know	18	22	15	17	18	21
There must be something in all the reports you hear	19	21	17	20	21	15
I just think there are such things	22	21	22	15	24	27
I don't really know	22	19	24	20	17	29
Has anyone close to you (as far as you know) ever encountered anything that they thought might be a ghost?						
Yes	20	20	19	27	21	13
No	32	36	28	30	31	32
Don't know	48	44	54	42	48	55
Have you ever encountered anything yourself which you thought might be a ghost?						
Yes	17	16	17	27	16	8
No	58	58	58	50	60	63
Don't know	25	26	25	23	24	29
If yes:						
Have you had that experience often, sometimes, occasionally, or just once?						
Often	49	47	50	54	46	45
Sometimes	21	21	21	12	24	31
Occasionally	19	18	21	21	19	16
Once only	11	14	8	13	11	9

things, while similar proportions believed because of reports from people known to them (18 per cent) or simply because they would not dismiss the nature of all the stories they had heard about these phenomena (19 per cent). Overall, one in five respondents (20 per cent) knew someone who had encountered something that they thought might be a ghost. Slightly fewer (17 per cent) said they themselves had experienced some such thing too. Among the latter, nearly half (49 per cent) said they had such experiences often. Younger respondents were more likely to claim ghostly experiences than were older respondents (see table 9.3)

BELIEF IN PARANORMAL AND PSYCHICAL POWERS

Finally, another aspect of the paranormal about which there is mixed public opinion is the existence of psychical powers. Is it possible that some people have the ability to predict the future, read minds, or sense things that are happening in the distant future? With regard to belief in psychical power, many young people were uncertain what to think. Nearly half (48 per cent) were unsure whether some people have the ability to foresee the future. More than half (52 per cent) were uncertain about telepathy and a similar proportion (49 per cent) did not know whether to believe that clairvoyance is possible. Somewhat fewer were unsure about spiritualism (42 per cent). Among those who committed themselves to an opinion, believers outnumbered non-believers with regard to seeing into the future (30 per cent versus 23 per cent) and with regard to clairvoyance (30 per cent versus 22 per cent). The proportions of believers and non-believers in telepathy were equal (24 per cent). Non-believers outnumbered believers in regard to spiritualism (33 per cent versus 26 per cent). Nearly one in four (24 per cent) claimed to have experienced a premonition themselves. Fewer claimed to have ever had a telepathic experience (14 per cent), a clairvoyant experience (16 per cent), or to have communicated through spiritualism with the dead (15 per cent). The youngest respondents were consistently the most likely to believe in paranormal and psychical powers (see table 9.4).

CONCLUDING REMARKS

While regular church attendance is on the decline, religious beliefs have far from disappeared. Most people attend formal religious

Table 9.4 Belief in paranormal and psychical powers

		Sex			Age	
	All %	Male %	Female %	10–14 %	15–16 %	17+ %
Do you think some people have the ability to foresee the future?						
Yes	30	31	28	28	33	26
No	22	25	20	24	23	19
Don't know	48	44	52	48	43	55
Have you ever had an experience like this yourself; such as a premonition that came true or a feeling or just knew what would happen?						
Yes	24	22	25	33	31	16
No	30	35	27	30	29	34
Don't know	46	43	48	37	40	50
Do you think there are people who can communicate with others, not by speaking, but just by thinking — that is, by what people sometimes call telepathy?						
Yes	24	21	26	30	25	18
No	24	28	20	24	27	21
Don't know	52	51	54	46	48	61
Have you yourself ever had an experience like this?						
Yes	14	12	16	19	16	7
No	71	73	68	66	70	75
Don't know	16	16	17	15	13	18
Some people have the ability to know about events that are happening, as they happen, even though they are taking place a long way away. This is sometimes called clairvoyance. Do you think this is possible?						
Yes	30	29	31	38	29	25
No	22	24	19	26	24	15
Don't know	48	47	50	36	47	61
Has anything like this ever happened to you?						
Yes	16	15	16	24	20	5
No	70	68	73	65	67	80
Don't know	14	17	11	11	14	16
Some people believe that it is possible to communicate with the dead — this is sometimes called spiritualism. Do you think such communication is possible or not?						
Yes	26	23	28	29	26	24
No	33	41	25	33	30	33
Don't know	41	36	47	38	43	43
Have you ever had such an experience?						
Yes	15	16	13	18	21	6
No	68	69	68	61	62	80
Don't know	17	15	19	21	17	14

ceremonies or services only occasionally. But many still indulge in private forms of worship and other religious or spiritual experiences. There is some evidence for Britain that the traditional, Christian-based religions together with their formal styles of worship have lost favour particularly with young people. This does not happen across the board among all young people, however, nor does it represent a generalized rejection of religious belief or a lack of any kind of spiritual involvement.

The indications from our survey are that young people today do associate themselves with a religion and hold religious beliefs. They do not, however, extensively engage in overt acts of worship or attendance at religious occasions. Most have at some time attended a religious ceremony on a special occasion, such as at Christmas or Easter or for a wedding or funeral. This sort of attendance is infrequent for most young people. Routine church attendance occurred only among a small minority of our respondents, most of whom had not attended even one service in the last year.

In connection with some special religious occasions, however, there was widespread uncertainty about attendance over the previous year. More than half could not remember for sure whether or not they had been to a wedding, funeral service, or religious festival during the past year. This uncertainty about church attendance may be one reflection of the relatively low level of importance attached to formal church-going by young people. Uncertainty about the frequency of attendance at regular religious services became more pronounced among older adolescents. This may indicate that, as they progress through their teenage years and gain greater independence and freedom to make up their own minds about religion, many young people decide not to attend church or other formal religious services. This observation is reinforced by the greater likelihood among older than among younger teenagers in our sample of thinking that attending a place of worship on a regular basis is not an important thing that they ought to do.

The fact that going to church was uncommon did not mean that religion was perceived as being unimportant. Many in our sample felt that religion was important to them. For some, religious experience was clearly a private thing. Prayer is one form of private religious worship. Only a minority said that they ever prayed, but among those who did many claimed to do so regularly on a daily basis. Praying regularly — as often as several times a day — was something much more likely to be claimed by respondents up to the age of 14 years than by older teenagers.

While religious experience of some sort was mentioned as important by many respondents, this was not reflected in a widespread belief in God or in some other supernatural being who has some influence over life's events. Some respondents held this belief, while others dismissed it. Many, however, were uncertain. A similar pattern of beliefs emerged in connection with the existence of an after-life and a heavenly world. Younger teenagers were more fateful in their outlook than older ones, and most likely to say they believed in God.

Many respondents, however, were unsure about the existence of an after-life or heavenly world. Among many young people, therefore, it seems that opinions and beliefs in this realm are not well-formed. This may reflect the fact that these are not matters to which they give much thought.

On the fringes of religious, spiritual, or psychical experience, some of our respondents claimed to believe in astrological predictions, ghosts, and paranormal phenomena. In general, though, sceptics outnumbered believers and any interest in these subjects seemed probably to stem from a fascination and curiosity about the unknown, the unexplained, and the mysterious.

Chapter Ten

HEALTH BELIEFS AND
THE ENVIRONMENT

With the development of social attitudes adolescents begin to think more deeply about a range of social and environmental issues. Industrial growth, nuclear power, expanded volumes of domestic traffic and international air travel have all been developments which have enhanced the standard of living around the world. At the same time, however, there has been a certain cost to the environment as each development brings its own particular kind of pollution. It should come as no surprise that concern about many pollutants is widespread among all age groups. Special concern might be expected among young people, though, because they have longer to live in this increasingly polluted and physically damaged world.

In addition to the 'health' of the environment, another area of apparently increasing concern, and certainly one which these days has attracted a growing emphasis, is that of personal health and fitness. Physical exercise and greater attention to one's diet have spawned growth industries. Health, however, seems often not to be a subject high on the agenda of young people, possibly because most of them rarely suffer from serious illness and take their health for granted. But, although most medical practice in western societies focuses on providing cures once health has been lost, there is a growing awareness that much can be done to prevent illness in the first place, at both a personal and a societal level. People can take care of their health better by making sure that they eat and drink sensibly, take plenty of exercise, and take time out from the stresses of everyday life to relax, physically and mentally. In this chapter, we examine young people's opinions about environmental pollution and personal health.

In an age of increasing concern about damage done to the environment by pollution caused by sources of power and energy, industrial processes, and traffic on land and in the air, we asked young people for their opinions about the seriousness of various known pollutants. In the first part of this chapter we present some of the results. Another area of increased concern among people today is that of personal health. We were interested to find out about young people's attitudes towards health and towards the efficacy of medical professionals and treatments to deal with illnesses. Finally, we examine the prevalence and nature of two behaviours known to have important implications for health, namely smoking and drinking.

BELIEFS CONCERNING ENVIRONMENTAL POLLUTION

We were concerned with six types of environmental pollution, with levels of concern about noise, fumes, and other forms of pollution. The items had previously been used in *British Social Attitudes* surveys (Jowell and Witherspoon 1985). The 1984 survey, for example, asked how serious an effect on the environment respondents felt resulted from aircraft noise, lead from petrol, industrial waste, waste from nuclear power stations, industrial fumes in the air, and noise and dirt from traffic. Most respondents proved to be concerned about most of these sources of pollution; 80 per cent of respondents thought that at least four of these sources had 'very' or 'quite serious' effects on the environment (Young 1985). The rank order in terms of percentages of respondents saying that each pollutant was 'very serious' was waste from nuclear power stations (69 per cent), industrial waste in rivers and sea (67 per cent), industrial fumes in the air (46 per cent), lead from petrol (45 per cent), noise and dirt from traffic (20 per cent), and noise from aircraft (7 per cent).

The 1985 survey (Jowell *et al.* 1986) found no large shifts in attitudes towards these issues compared with previous years, but there did seem to have been a slight diminution of concern about most of these threats to the quality of the environment, as more respondents in 1985 classified various hazards as 'quite serious' rather than 'very serious' compared with 1984. There was a marked decline in concern about nuclear waste, which was consistent with responses noted elsewhere in the survey to a series of questions on nuclear issues (Young 1986). This was an interesting finding because the past year had seen a considerable increase in the salience of nuclear energy issues, with most of the publicity not being favourable.

The general slackening of concern about nuclear waste was apparent among both men and women of all age groups, with the exception perhaps of younger men. The very high levels of concern expressed by younger women in 1984 were much less apparent, while among men aged 35 to 54 decline in concern was particularly steep. Nor were these shifts merely changes of emphasis at the 'most concerned' end of the response categories offered. In 1984, 90 per cent of middle-aged men and 93 per cent of younger women registered high levels of concern, believing that nuclear waste had either a very serious or a quite serious effect on the environment. In 1985, the corresponding figures were 76 per cent and 89 per cent.

We turn now to the results of our youth survey. In rank order according to how many youth respondents thought each one has a serious effect on the environment, the environmental pollutants lined up as shown in table 10.1. The pollutant most often perceived as either quite or very serious was waste from nuclear power stations (85 per cent), with many respondents (65 per cent) saying this was a very serious problem. Nearly nine out of ten (88 per cent) thought that industrial waste in the rivers and the sea was at least quite a serious problem, with slightly fewer (62 per cent) saying it was very serious compared with nuclear waste. More than eight out of ten (82 per cent) thought that industrial fumes in the air posed a serious environmental threat and almost as many (80 per cent) were worried about lead from petrol.

Of less concern were noise and dirt from traffic although even here a majority of respondents (62 per cent) saw this as a problem, and noise from aircraft (36 per cent). By and large, both male and female respondents perceived these pollutants to be serious problems to an equal extent. The extent to which serious concern was endorsed increased with age in connection with nearly every form of environmental pollutant.

OPINIONS CONCERNING PORNOGRAPHY

Opinions concerning the availability of pornographic magazines and films revealed a mixture of viewpoints, some pro- and others anti-censorship. At the two extremes, the views either that such materials should be banned altogether or that they should be available in any shop for sale to anyone were endorsed equally (by 17 per cent).

Table 10.1 Beliefs concerning environmental pollution

How serious an effect on our environment do you think each of these things has?

	All %	Male %	Female %
Waste from nuclear power stations			
Very serious	65	63	65
Quite serious	20	17	24
Not very serious	9	10	8
Not at all serious	7	10	4
Industrial waste in rivers/sea			
Very serious	62	64	60
Quite serious	26	22	24
Not very serious	7	7	9
Not at all serious	6	6	6
Industrial fumes in the air			
Very serious	50	50	50
Quite serious	32	30	33
Not very serious	13	14	13
Not at all serious	5	6	4
Lead from petrol			
Very serious	41	43	39
Quite serious	39	37	42
Not very serious	14	14	14
Not at all serious	6	6	6
Noise and dirt from traffic			
Very serious	22	27	17
Quite serious	40	38	42
Not very serious	29	26	32
Not at all serious	9	10	9
Noise from aircraft			
Very serious	13	18	10
Quite serious	23	24	22
Not very serious	46	37	52
Not at all serious	19	22	17

Table 10.2 Beliefs concerning environmental pollution as a function of age and class

	Age			Class		
	10–14	*15–16*	*17 +*	*ABC1*	*C2*	*DE*
	%	%	%	%	%	%
Noise from aircraft						
Very serious	20	12	8	10	14	13
Quite serious	25	17	27	25	20	29
Not very serious	38	51	46	49	43	42
Not at all serious	17	21	19	16	23	16
Lead from petrol						
Very serious	40	41	41	45	39	41
Quite serious	39	41	39	40	39	39
Not very serious	12	14	16	10	16	18
Not at all serious	9	5	4	6	6	2
Industrial waste in rivers/sea						
Very serious	56	59	68	63	57	75
Quite serious	27	27	25	24	29	23
Not very serious	10	7	5	7	8	2
Not at all serious	7	7	3	7	6	0
Waste from nuclear power stations						
Very serious	63	60	70	65	60	84
Quite serious	23	24	15	21	22	7
Not very serious	6	9	10	7	10	9
Not at all serious	8	7	5	8	7	0
Industrial fumes in the air						
Very serious	47	49	54	51	48	59
Quite serious	32	34	30	34	31	27
Not very serious	14	13	14	10	16	14
Not at all serious	7	5	3	6	4	0
Noise and dirt from traffic						
Very serious	17	20	26	19	21	34
Quite serious	44	37	41	42	39	41
Not very serious	30	34	24	30	30	23
Not at all serious	10	8	10	9	10	2

Most respondents opted for one of two less extreme opinions. Just over one in four (27 per cent) felt that pornographic material should be available in special adult shops but not displayed to the public, while one in three (31 per cent) felt that pornography should be available in any shop, but that sales should be restricted to adults only.

Females exhibited more conservative opinions than males. More females (23 per cent) than males (12 per cent) in this youth sample wanted to have pornography banned altogether. And males (19 per cent) more often than females (13 per cent) felt that pornography should be available on sale any time to anyone.

Table 10.3 Opinions concerning pornography

	All %	*Male* %	*Female* %
Which of these statements comes closest to your views on the availability of pornographic magazines and films?			
They should be banned altogether	17	12	23
They should be available in special adult shops but not displayed to the public	27	28	26
They should be available in special adult shops with public display permitted	9	8	11
They should be available in any shop for sale to adults only	31	33	26
They should be available in any shop for sale to anyone	17	19	13

HEALTH MATTERS

These days, diet, exercise, and other health-related matters have become a major public preoccupation. They are topics frequently discussed in the media and, with the expansion of leisure time available to most people today, have generated a successful tertiary industry.

Our health is understandably one of the most, if not the most, important things in life. Without it, we cannot function properly and enjoy life to the full. It has been said by some, however, that this increased preoccupation with health has also produced an associated rise in concern about illness. Some doctors believe that the health fads of recent years have triggered hypochondriasis in those predisposed to develop this neurosis. But what do people, and in particular young people, think about health and illness? Do they perceive themselves to be in good health or not? Do they believe that good health is a matter of good luck or that it can be influenced by attitude of mind and by life-style? And do they have faith in the competence of the medical profession to provide help or cures when one's health fails?

When asked if, on the whole, they felt that they had good health or not, a substantial majority (79 per cent) said that they did not know. Just under one in ten (9 per cent) felt they had good health and a few more than this (12 per cent) felt that their health was not good. Males (75 per cent) were less likely than females (81 per cent) to say they did not know if they had good health.

In the event that a person's health has failed them completely, and they have acquired a painful, unbearable disease, should doctors be empowered by law to end that patient's life (and suffering) if the patient requests it? Nearly three out of four youth respondents (72 per cent) felt that this should not be allowed, with males (71 per cent) and females (73 per cent) in almost complete agreement.

Should a doctor also be permitted by law to end the life of someone who is simply tired of living and who requires a way out? Although rejection of this idea was not as widespread, nevertheless nearly two out of three respondents (63 per cent) felt that this should not be allowed, and 37 per cent said it should be allowed.

There was a substantial difference of opinion between males and females on this question, however. Males were equally divided (50 per cent–50 per cent) between accepting and rejecting the idea of euthanasia for someone who is tired of living, whereas females were three to one against the idea.

OPINIONS ABOUT HEALTH CARE AND MEDICAL TREATMENT

Research has indicated that people differ in the extent to which they consider they are in control of their health and that the nature of this belief can influence their own recovery from illness and whether they think medical efforts are important or ineffective in the treatment of illness or injury (King 1982). These 'health locus of control' beliefs seem to be related also to the extent to which individuals keep careful checks on their health (Strickland 1978). Research has also indicated that internal health controllers express stronger intentions to seek out health-related information than do external health controllers, but that such beliefs do not relate to actual information-seeking behaviour (De Vito *et al.* 1982; Wallston *et al.* 1976).

Respondents were given twelve items which expressed beliefs about the causes of health and recovery from illness which were derived from the Health Locus of Control Scale (Lau 1982). The results in table 10.4 show the extent to which respondents agreed or disagreed with each statement.

Strong or fairly strong agreement was predominant on seven out of the twelve items. A majority of respondents at least quite agreed that good health depends on good luck (81 per cent). At the same time, though, a degree of perceived personal control over health was apparent. Most respondents felt that if they got sick, they themselves were usually to blame (75 per cent) and for others, too, ill-health tended to result from their own carelessness (71 per cent).

Once you get ill, then you have problems. More than three out of four (78 per cent) believed there isn't much you can do for yourself when you get sick. Getting well, so most of these young people believed, depends on good fortune. Many (40 per cent) rejected the idea that recovery from illness has nothing to do with luck, and many more (29 per cent) could only agree weakly with this belief. But despite this, there was relatively modest agreement with the statement that, no matter what anybody does, there are many diseases that can just wipe you out. Nearly one in three (31 per cent) rejected this belief, while a similar proportion (33 per cent) could only agree with it to some extent. More than half (53 per cent) believed at least quite strongly that there are few diseases today that are totally crippling. Just over 16 per cent could not agree with this.

What about doctors and the help they can provide? In general, youth respondents exhibited little confidence in the medical profession and the efficacy of medical treatment to help recovery from illness. Half the respondents said that they strongly agreed with the statement that doctors can rarely do very much for people who are sick and a further one in five (21 per cent) said that they quite agreed with this. Most (70 per cent) believed that doctors relieve or cure only a few of the medical problems of their patients, while there was only modest agreement that doctors can almost always help their patients to feel better. One in three (31 per cent) did not agree at all that most people are helped a great deal when they go to a doctor, while a similar proportion (33 per cent) only agreed mildly.

147

Table 10.4 Opinions about health care and medical treatment

	Strongly Agree %	Quite Agree %	Somewhat Agree %	Do not Agree %
Good health is largely a matter of good luck	59	22	13	6
Doctors can rarely do very much for people who are sick	50	21	17	11
Healthwise, there isn't much you can do for yourself when you get sick	48	30	13	9
If I get sick, it's usually my own fault	44	31	17	8
Doctors relieve or cure only a few of the medical problems that their patients have	33	37	22	8
People's ill-health results from their own carelessness	30	41	21	8
In today's world few diseases are totally crippling	20	33	31	16
No matter what anybody does, there are many diseases that can just wipe you out	13	24	33	31
Doctors can almost always help their patients to feel better	10	28	38	24
Recovery from illness has nothing to do with luck	8	22	29	40
Most people are helped a great deal when they go to a doctor	8	28	33	31
In the long run, people who take good care of themselves stay healthy and get well speedily	6	21	39	34

MISCELLANEOUS HEALTH-RELATED BELIEF

More respondents agreed (50 per cent) than disagreed (30 per cent) that contraceptive advice and supplies should be available to all young people whatever their age, and 20 per cent did not know. This pattern was reversed with respect to opinions about legalized cannabis (marijuana) smoking. Fewer agreed (30 per cent) than disagreed

(51 per cent) that this should be allowed. One in five (19 per cent) neither agreed nor disagreed. There was a difference of opinion among males and females on this item, however. Females (27 per cent) agreed less often than males (36 per cent) that cannabis smoking should be legalized.

The use of animals for experimental purposes has for a long time been a controversial and contentious issue. Opinions given here indicate that how acceptable it is to use animals in laboratory tests depends on what the tests are for. For these young people, using animals for testing and improving cosmetics (59 per cent disagreement against 15 per cent agreement with 17 per cent uncertain) was less acceptable than for testing medicines if it could save human lives (37 per cent disagreement against 44 per cent agreement and 19 per cent uncertain). Once again, males and females differed in their opinions. Males (51 per cent) were more often accepting of the use of animals for laboratory tests, especially for medical purposes, than were females (32 per cent).

SMOKING AND DRINKING HABITS

In rounding off our look at young people's health-related beliefs and behaviour, we examine their claimed smoking and drinking habits. Several studies of smoking prevalence have been carried out among UK adolescent and youth samples in recent years. Gillies *et al.* (1987) reported a survey of over 45,000 teenagers from 269 schools in the Trent region of England. Questionnaires which asked about smoking habits were completed in the classroom. The survey found that one in five 15–16–year–olds, and more girls (23 per cent) than boys (18 per cent), were regular smokers. Although not actually at the same level, according to the researchers this result confirmed the high prevalence of regular smoking in 15–16–year–olds nationally. An earlier study had recorded an average of 30 per cent for England and Wales as a whole in 1984 (Dobbs and Marsh 1985). Two further international surveys, which included samples from the UK, both found that weekly smoking levels among teenagers were somewhat lower than those indicated by the above findings, though substantial numbers of young people had at one time or another experimented with smoking (Aaro *et al.* 1986; Boddewyn 1986).

Seven out of ten respondents in our survey (70 per cent) claimed to have smoked a cigarette at some time; males (71 per cent) were very slightly more likely to have done so than females (67 per cent). When asked if they smoked cigarettes these days, just under four out of ten (42 per cent) said that they did. Here, females (43 per cent) slightly outnumbered males (40 per cent).

Those adolescents who claimed to be smokers were asked about how many cigarettes they smoked in an average day. One in three (33 per cent) claimed to smoke less than five a day, one in three (34 per cent) six to ten a day, and the remainder (32 per cent) more than ten a day. Females were less heavy smokers than males.

Experience with alcoholic drinks was more widespread than smoking. Practically all respondents (98 per cent) claimed to have had an alcoholic drink at some time. Most had had a drink at home (96 per cent), whereas fewer had drunk alcohol in a public house (78 per cent). One in three (31 per cent) claimed to drink at home most weeks, while one in four (24 per cent) said they went to the pub for a drink at least several times a week. Males were more likely than females to claim to drink frequently at home (41 per cent versus 22 per cent) and at least several times a week at a pub (31 per cent versus 15 per cent).

CONCLUDING REMARKS

Our focus in this chapter has been upon young people's concern about environmental pollutants and personal health matters. The two can conceivably be linked in various ways, though in our survey they were investigated as separate areas of opinion.

Under 'pollutants' we considered physical damage to the natural environment created by the waste products of industrial, energy, and traffic sources and also the social 'pollution' of pornography. In both cases, there was an element of concern among our respondents.

The most serious damage to the physical environment was thought to be caused by nuclear power and industrial waste. Traffic-related waste, although of some concern, was perceived less often as very serious. Male respondents were more likely to be seriously concerned than were female respondents about noise and dirt from traffic and noise from aircraft, while both sexes exhibited widespread marked concern for other pollutants. Concerns about industrial and nuclear waste grow with age. The survey was carried out pre-Chernobyl, so it may be predicted that concern about the waste products from nuclear power stations will have become even more prevalent among young people since then.

On the subject of social pollution as caused by pornography, a mixture of opinions was forthcoming. Some respondents were in favour of censorship, others were not. Equal proportions supported total banning and unrestricted availability. Most respondents, however, endorsed either of two less extreme measures which both involved some degree of control over availability. Females were more supportive of restrictions on the availability of pornography than males.

On health matters, we were interested to find out about how healthy respondents thought themselves, about the perceived efficacy of professional medical treatment for ill-health, and the extent to which people are seen to be themselves responsible for their own health and recovery from illness.

By a ratio of 3 to 1, our respondents were against allowing doctors to end the life of someone with an incurable illness, but this was reduced to a 2 to 1 ratio in favour of allowing euthanasia for the incurably sick if they themselves request it. However, there was a marked sex difference on the latter opinion. Females were widely against allowing people to request having their own life ended, while males were equally divided between being for and against it.

Awareness of personal state of health was not very extensive among our youth sample. Around three out of four did not know whether they had good or poor health. Good health was perceived to be a matter both of good fortune and personal responsibility. Many respondents felt that illness could often be avoided through careful attention to one's own health.

Problems begin following the onset of illness, however. Most of our youth sample believed that there is not much you can do for yourself when you get sick. Furthermore, our respondents revealed little confidence in the health profession effectively to aid recovery from illness. There was a pervasive belief that doctors can rarely do much for people once they are ill and that it is only sometimes that the sick are helped to any great extent by the medical profession.

The smoking and drinking claims of our sample revealed that, although a large majority had experimented with cigarettes, less than half currently smoked. Drinking alcoholic beverages, however, was much more widespread. Regular drinking among those who did partake was more commonplace than regular smoking among the smokers.

Chapter Eleven

ATTITUDES TO SCHOOL, WORK, AND UNEMPLOYMENT

Certainly two of the areas that adolescents have strong beliefs about are schooling and employment. The vast majority of our sample were at school though these ranged enormously in type, size, orientation, etc. Many studies in different countries have looked at adolescents' attitudes to various aspects of their school life and we were interested in asking our sample some of these questions. But adolescence is also a time of expectation and transition and one of the most important concerns the world of work or, for the less fortunate, the experience of unemployment.

In this chapter, then, we will focus on such things as how scholars believe they should behave in school and their perception of the importance of education; beliefs about getting a job; perceptions of the nature of inflation and unemployment and finally about how to get most out of one's work.

ATTITUDES TO WORK

Are young people as work-orientated as their parents? Is the work ethic on the decline? What sort of jobs are young people looking for?

We attempted to measure young people's work values, and more specifically the extent to which they ascribed to the work ethic values and ideals. A very great deal has been written about the work ethic — whether it ever existed, whether it accounted for the origins of capitalism, or whether it is on the decline (Furnham 1988). We decided to give our sample a simple eight-item questionnaire devised by Blood (1969) to measure work ethic values like — hard work brings rewards, occupational achievement brings prestige, etc. These questions which have been used in many studies have been shown to be related to many aspects of job satisfaction, indeed satisfaction with life in general.

A second topic of interest concerns what sort of job our youth sample were looking for — specifically what dimensions or facets of the job they rated most and least highly. A whole range of factors have been thought to relate to job satisfaction, such as challenging work, job security, pay, autonomy and responsibility, concerned supervision, good physical working conditions, etc. Results of many studies have shown two particularly interesting findings: the first is that most people are quite satisfied with their jobs and that this pattern has not really changed over the years such that reported satisfaction has neither increased nor decreased greatly in recent decades. It is known that job satisfaction rises with age and status but a second important finding is that pay is almost never the first (second or third) factor nominated as the major cause of satisfaction or dissatisfaction; pay is only one factor and very frequently not the most important. Hence, we were very interested in finding out what our sample believed were the most desirable aspects or facets of a job.

GETTING A JOB

Since the mid- to late-1970s when the problem became most acute in nearly every developed country, there have been a number of important studies on youth unemployment. The underlying causes are, of course, manifold, and include demographic factors (changes in the birth rate and an extension of the school career); micro- and macro-economic changes (introduction of new technology, new productivity agreements); as well as educational and training factors (the relevance and perceived appropriateness of education). Changes in youth unemployment move with greater amplitude than those of adults. Indeed, in Britain it has been calculated that if the unemployment rate for males rises by 1 per cent, the unemployment rate for young males under 20 years excluding school leavers rises by 1.7 per cent (Makeham 1980).

In a review of the work on youth unemployment, Furnham (1985c) has divided the literature into various sections:

Psychological adjustment

Many studies from different countries have tended to show that, compared to school-leavers who have found jobs, unemployed young people tend to be more anxious and depressed, have lower self-esteem and subjective well-being, are less socially adjusted.

The problem with nearly all the studies on youth unemployment and psychological adjustment is that one cannot infer cause — only correlation. That is, it is quite possible that poor psychological adjustment leads to a young person being unemployed, rather than the other way around.

Banks and Jackson (1982) interviewed two age cohorts of young people up to two-and-a-half years after leaving school to investigate the association between unemployment and the risk of minor psychiatric morbidity. They found a positive relationship between unemployment and disturbance after controlling for sex, ethnic group, and educational qualifications. Further longitudinal analyses showed that the experience of unemployment was more likely to create increased psychological symptoms, rather than the reverse. More recently, Jackson *et al.* (1983) studied longitudinally two cohorts of young people in the first three years of their working lives. They found, as predicted, that psychological distress is higher for the unemployed than for the employed, and that changes in employment status lead to changes in distress score. Furthermore, this relationship is moderated by the person's commitment to work — the more committed suffer more from the experience of unemployment.

Education about unemployment

A number of researchers, particularly in the area of career and vocational guidance, have been interested in education about the possibility of unemployment rather than employment.

Darcy (1978) has argued that young people need to be educated in all aspects of job-sharing and to be encouraged to have a new definition of work, to include not only paid employment but a variety of other activities. Hence, a careers education programme should involve such topics as the mechanics of collecting benefits, the acquisition of job-seeking skills, the experience of unemployment, the leisure and community roles, and the politics of the right to work. Watts (1978) also considered the implications of school-leaver unemployment for careers education in schools. He argues that careers educators have not seriously dealt with the problem of unemployment because they do not feel competent to tackle it effectively; because they are aware of its highly political and emotional overtones; because it might affect deleteriously the work ethic within and outside the school; and because the teachers feel instinctively hostile to the concept of preparation for unemployment. A number of possible curricular objectives are listed, including equipping children with employability, survival, and leisure skills. Four alternative aims are described, depending on whether one is focusing on change in society (to help students see unemployment as a phenomenon resolved by social and political measures); change in the individual (to maximize students' chances of finding meaningful employment); status quo in the society (to reinforce students' motivation to seek work); and status quo in the individual (to make students aware of the possibility of unemployment and how to best cope with it). Many of the educational responses and strategies are dependent on whether one believes unemployment to be voluntary (aversion of the will to work), cyclical (cycles of recession and expansion), or structural (a major change in the relationship between capital and labour). Solutions may include a deeper inculcation of the work ethic, job creation schemes, etc. Careers education is seen as the education of central life interests and personal growth and development, rather than the matching of people to (non-existent) jobs.

Job interview training

One consequence of mass youth unemployment has been a focusing of attention on job interview skills. Many researchers have become aware of the fact that because of skill deficits on the part of both interviewers and interviewees, potentially able candidates were getting rejected because of their poor social performance in the job interview rather than their inability to actually perform the task. Hood *et al.* (1982) allocated school leavers to either an interview-training or a discussion control group. The interview-training group received a combination of modelling coaching, role play, feedback, and discussion to train both verbal and non-verbal interview skills. Later, the school leavers were assessed using video-taped, role-played interviews which were made at the beginning and the end of each training phase. The trained group showed significant improvements on global, as well as specific, ratings — question asking and answering, fidgeting, smiling, eye contact, gesture, posture, and interest — compared to the control group. The researchers demonstrated the generalization and maintenance of these treatment effects over time. In conclusion they noted:

Studies that have been concerned with interview training for various populations of adolescents indicated that such training may have a worthwhile contribution to make in preparing them for seeking employment. In view of the current employment situation, performance in the interview is more critical than ever before and interview training may fulfil a preventive function in interrupting the process of failure in interview, lack of work experience, and further failure in interview, before it becomes entrenched and leads to other psychological problems. (Hood *et al.* 1982: 592)

Explanations and expectations about employment and unemployment

Many studies have shown that the expectations young people have of finding a job (as well as their job search behaviour) actually determine whether they find a job or not *and* how they subsequently explain it.

Research within the framework of attribution theory would, however, lead one to make a number of predictions about school children's expectations. Those more prone to unemployment, and the unemployed themselves, tend to make more external attributions for the causes of unemployment, in contrast to those in jobs and unlikely to become unemployed. Furthermore, studies have shown that external attributions are to some extent protective of self-esteem in the context of achievement. Hence, Furnham (1984b) predicted that females more than males and working-class subjects more than middle-class subjects — for whom unemployment is statistically more probable — will be prone to make more external attributions about getting a job. Further, it was suggested that these attributions will also be reflected in the number and type of job-search strategies adopted by young people and the barriers and aids that they consider operate in job-hunting success. In this study, Furnham set out to examine sex and class differences in 240 British school leavers' attributions about unemployment, the most and least useful job-search strategies, and which school course they believed most and least useful in getting a job. The results of the four different parts of this study suggest that, overall, attributions about getting a job are frequently internal (i.e., to personal attributes or abilities rather than to environmental or societal factors). Confidence, perseverance, and qualifications were all considered to be primary factors responsible for success in finding employment, yet this is moderated by the belief that jobs are not currently available (a fact which is attributed to the government). Yet failure to get a job was rarely attributed to the personal short-comings of the job-seeker himself. Thus, these results tend to support the well-established, attributional finding that success is attributed to internal factors and failure to external factors.

Job search

Another crucial feature concerning youth employment and unemployment concerns how people set about trying to get a job. In the United States, Dayton (1981) looked at the way in which young people looked for a job. He set out to determine what job-seeking approaches were being used by young people and what factors they found positive and useful (aids) and what negative and worthless (barriers) in a job search. Using a population of 250 young Americans, Dayton found they regarded their own positive personal attributes (personality, flexibility, academic ability) as the most important aids in their job search, and external factors (labour unions, welfare and unemployment insurance, government training programmes) as least important. Employment success and satisfaction was correlated with careful analysis of which job suited them best, the assemblance of a placement file, letters of recommendation, and a c.v., combined with persistence in the job search.

Furnham (1984b) confirmed these results in Britain by finding that the young people saw their own personal attributes as the greatest aids and external factors as the biggest hindrances. Regarding the various strategies, class and sex differences showed that the middle class tended to rate all job-hunting strategies as more useful than the working class, and girls showed less faith in following up specific job choices than boys. The subjects all stressed the importance of summer and after-school work for experience, but tended to rely on personal contacts rather than direct approaches to employers. It would be interesting to compare these beliefs with those of employers, who may have quite different beliefs concerning which factors make an applicant more employable. The belief in the usefulness of A-level courses revealed that both males and females believed science courses (and English) were the most useful in getting a job, although females tended to opt for arts courses and males for science at A-level. Females also believed that arts courses were more useful than science courses, so providing a rationalization for the choice.

ATTITUDES TO SCHOOL

Both questionnaire and interview studies of young people's attitudes to school have shown that consistent themes recur. They are also to be found in written essays that scholars are compelled so frequently and reluctantly to complete. Some of the issues that frequently occur include the following:

rules and discipline — this issue concerns the fairness and appropriateness of rules and the punishments which ensue when they are broken; often debates occur around issues such as who devises and implements rules as well as the necessity of rules for the protection of certain rights;

teachers — although there is a wide range of issues within this category the most frequently occurring issues appear to be teacher competence (with respect to experience, knowledge, and qualifications) as well as communication skills such as being approachable, helpful, and understanding; a related issue involves within and outside class teacher-student relationships;

buildings and equipment — this refers to all aspects of the school facilities such as sporting facilities (swimming pools, libraries) as well as such things as class furniture;

general educational issues — again this includes many issues such as class sizes, co-education, homework and examinations, continuous assessment, more free time, etc.; nearly always these issues concern change from the present scheme to some other system thought to be more favourable.

There is a host of other issues that we could have asked children about school and their expectations and experiences. However, in the limited space available we were interested in some specific issues highlighted by Poole (1983):

'*not breaking the boundaries*' — that is, a conformity to the status quo and having relatively low expectations of what one might expect from a school;

the value of schooling — whether school is essentially a waste of time or whether it provides training in independence and careers selection; this also concerns how much adolescents expect from schools and the extent to which they are fed up or bored with schooling;

school curriculum and innovation — this concerns issues such as methods of assessment, changes in the sort of things that are taught, etc.; *teachers* — finally we asked two questions about their attitude to teachers.

Poole concluded thus:

Overall, students believed that it was important to plan their careers and future lives. Goal setting was seen as important, as was hard work. In addition, most students believe their education was of value and that more of it led to better life changes. . . Adolescents expected their schools to provide them with training in independence and in job choice. Females placed greater value on schooling than did males, as did students in independent schools. . . As to the school curriculum and the methods of learning, most students enjoyed planning their own work, wanted more diverse offerings and practical courses. Some 60% of adolescents felt they would like to attend school part-time and work a few days a week. There was some evidence of other-orientation and altruism in students eg. many were willing to work for the community — or to help friends. Attitudes to teachers were mixed. (Poole 1983: 109)

We have arranged the results of this chapter into just five sections: expectations about inflation and unemployment; attitudes to work; the perceived most and least important aspects of a job; beliefs about getting a job; attitudes to school.

INFLATION AND UNEMPLOYMENT

We first asked our sample four relatively simple questions about inflation and unemployment over the coming year. Despite the fact that the inflation rate was between 4 and 8 per cent when the data were collected, nearly half (47 per cent) expected prices to go up *a lot* and a third (36 per cent) expected them to go up a little. This effect was marked by an age difference with older children (50 per cent) expecting inflation more than younger children (43 per cent), though this may simply be a reflection of the former's greater experience of economic affairs.

Over two-thirds also believed that unemployment would go up either a lot (36 per cent) or a little (33 per cent) which was also fairly surprising as the data were gathered when official figures suggested unemployment had, in effect, stabilized and was, if anything, moving down. About 10 per cent said it would stay the same and 13 per cent go down a little. Again there was a strong age difference with older children (55 per cent) expecting greater unemployment than younger children (27 per cent).

Asked which priority they believed the government should follow by trying to keep either inflation *or* unemployment down, almost three times as many said unemployment (59 per cent) as inflation (22 per cent), which was against the major policies of the government of the day (14 per cent said they did not know). Older children (7 per cent) were less uncertain than younger children (30 per cent) and tended to opt for one or other response rather than don't know.

The general feeling of pessimism, however, did not extend to a general evaluation of Britain's performance over the following year in which one in three (30 per cent) expected some improvement, over one in three that things would stay much the same, and only 14 per cent that things would decline. Eight per cent believed there would be a lot of improvement and 11 per cent did not know.

ATTITUDES TO WORK

Of the eight statements we offered four were broadly in favour of the Protestant work ethic and four broadly against it. The fact the adolescents tended to respond favourably to both sets of questions indicated that they favour a work-hard/play-hard philosophy rather than the work-accepting, leisure-rejecting ethic of the strict work ethic.

In all, 85 per cent agreed that after the working day a person should put their job behind them and attempt to enjoy themselves but 64 per cent thought hard work made one a better person. Approximately half of our youth sample agreed with the pro-work ethic statements, 'Wasting time is as bad as wasting money' and 'A good indication of a person's worth is how well they do at their job'.

Whereas there were fewer than expected sex or class differences nearly all statements with pro-and anti-work ethic items showed older respondents agreeing more than younger respondents. One of the biggest differences was on the somewhat fatalistic item which said people should accept life as it is rather than striving for unreachable goals (see table 11.1).

Table 11.1 Attitudes to work

		All %	10–14 %	Age 15–16 %	17 + %
When the work day is finished a person should forget his/her job and enjoy him/herself	Agree	85	77	89	88
	Neither	10	16	6	8
	Disagree	5	7	5	4
Hard work makes someone a better person	Agree	54	53	61	49
	Neither	30	35	25	32
	Disagree	16	12	14	19
The principal purpose of a person's job is to provide them with the means for enjoying their free time	Agree	50	41	59	46
	Neither	30	45	23	23
	Disagree	20	14	18	31
Wasting time is as bad as wasting money	Agree	49	44	51	54
	Neither	32	40	27	30
	Disagree	19	16	22	16
Wherever possible a person should relax and accept life as it is, rather than always striving for unreachable goals	Agree	55	48	52	67
	Neither	24	34	26	10
	Disagree	21	18	22	23
A good indication of a person's worth is how well they do at their job	Agree	50	46	49	56
	Neither	30	39	29	21
	Disagree	20	15	22	23
If all other things are equal, it is better to have a job with a lot of responsibility than one with little responsibility	Agree	46	44	48	46
	Neither	40	47	36	36
	Disagree	14	9	16	18
People who 'do things the easy way' are the smart ones	Agree	36	35	31	38
	Neither	28	34	25	17
	Disagree	36	31	44	45

THE PERCEIVED MOST AND LEAST IMPORTANT ASPECTS OF A JOB

We were particularly interested in our youth sample's perceptions of the major sources of job satisfaction. They were, in order, job security (72 per cent); satisfying work (62 per cent); good working conditions (61 per cent); pleasant work colleagues (56 per cent); career development (53 per cent); salary (39 per cent); responsibility (25 per cent); working hours (22 per cent). This is very much in line with the results obtained from adults which show that job security and intrinsic features of the job are more important than wages or hours.

There was also a range of very interesting age differences. Con-

Table 11.2 The most important aspects of a job

What do you think are the most important things to look for in a job?

	Very important				Quite important				Not very important				Not at all important			
		Age				Age				Age				Age		
	All	10–14	15–16	17+	All	10–14	15–16	17+	All	10–14	15–16	17+	All	10–14	15–16	17+
High starting wage or salary	39	44	44	23	43	37	38	57	18	17	17	20	0	2	1	0
Secure job for the future	72	64	76	75	21	25	21	21	5	9	3	4	2	2	0	0
Opportunities for career development	53	42	57	63	33	35	32	32	12	19	10	5	1	4	1	0
Satisfying work	62	46	64	80	29	38	30	18	5	10	4	2	4	6	2	0
Good working conditions	61	53	59	71	27	25	33	24	11	21	8	5	1	1	0	0
Pleasant people to work with	56	47	57	64	34	37	35	29	7	11	6	7	3	5	2	0
Short working hours	22	23	20	21	28	28	31	25	40	36	38	48	10	13	11	6
A lot of responsibility	25	32	25	16	35	32	36	41	29	28	27	33	11	8	12	10

There are certain groups who some people feel ought to be given favourable treatment when applying for jobs. Which of the following kinds of people do you think should be given special treatment?

	Should be given special treatment	Should not be given special treatment
Women	70	30
Black people	80	20
People with disabilities	28	72

sidering only the response 'very important', a clear and dramatic pattern arises. Older adolescents, many of whom were in work, rated starting wage and responsibility much *lower* than the younger children and in turn rated career development, satisfying work, working conditions, and job security much higher.

It seems that younger children believe extrinsic features of a job are more important than intrinsic features but that as they get older they tend to appreciate intrinsic features, more especially the nature of the work and colleagues at work.

We also asked if they believed certain groups should be given special or favourable treatment when applying for jobs. Eighty per cent agreed that blacks and 70 per cent that women should receive special treatment but less than a third (28 per cent) felt this should be given to disabled or handicapped people. This may come as a source of comfort to minority groups campaigning against negative discrimination and in favour of positive discrimination but as a source of distress to those groups who maintain that disabled people's major handicap is the attitudes of non-disabled people towards them (see table 11.2).

GETTING A JOB

How does one find a job in times of high unemployment? Is it a matter of luck or chance or a matter of effort and ability? To what extent does it help to have important or influential people pull strings for one? We were interested in what our youth sample thought were the main factors in obtaining work. However, as most of our sample was still at school and had not started the job search, about a third felt unable to either agree or disagree with these questions that they probably had not considered or were beyond their experience.

Most of the questions that concerned effort, ability, and qualification were agreed with by the majority who expressed an opinion: 65 per cent agreed that young people get jobs if they look hard, are confident, and have a lot to offer; 50 per cent agreed that people will get a job if well qualified; 48 per cent agreed that smarter young people get work; 52 per cent agreed that young people get work if they look hard and often enough.

Questions referring to chance and luck factors revealed rather mixed answers. For instance, 57 per cent agree that it is mainly luck whether a school leaver gets a job and 52 per cent believed that getting a job is mainly a matter of being at the right place at the right time. But

Table 11.3 Getting a job

		All %	10–14 %	Age 15–16 %	17 + %
It is mainly a matter of luck	Agree	57	57	57	57
whether a school-leaver gets a	Neither	17	20	12	17
job or not	Disagree	26	23	31	26
If they had better qualifications	Agree	46	52	51	23
most of the unemployed would	Neither	20	30	17	16
soon get jobs	Disagree	34	18	32	61
Most young people get jobs if	Agree	65	57	70	65
they look hard, are confident	Neither	21	32	19	14
and have a lot to offer	Disagree	14	11	11	21
Most school-leavers who have	Agree	40	45	40	40
got a job had somecne	Neither	30	35	25	29
'pulling strings' for them	Disagree	30	20	35	31
Getting a job is mainly a matter	Agree	52	35	55	69
of being in the right place at	Neither	26	40	23	16
the right time	Disagree	22	25	22	15
Unemployment is running so high	Agree	61	52	63	65
because the jobs simply are not	Neither	20	31	15	17
there	Disagree	19	17	22	18
It is mainly 'smarter' young	Agree	48	43	52	50
people who have been able to	Neither	29	40	27	21
get work	Disagree	23	17	21	29
Unemployed young people	Agree	36	38	41	25
haven't tried hard enough and	Neither	28	35	26	24
don't know how to sell themselves	Disagree	36	27	33	51
Young people miss out on getting	Agree	47	47	45	44
jobs because employers are	Neither	28	36	27	24
prejudiced against them	Disagree	25	17	29	32
If you miss out on getting work	Agree	25	30	29	15
it is because you are not good	Neither	27	39	25	18
enough	Disagree	48	31	46	67
Young people get work if they	Agree	52	48	58	52
look hard and often enough	Neither	25	38	21	20
	Disagree	23	14	21	32
The government is to blame for	Agree	52	49	60	54
young people being out of work	Neither	30	34	24	32
	Disagree	18	17	16	14
Getting a job depends on sheer	Agree	32	32	31	31
good luck	Neither	31	36	25	33
	Disagree	37	32	44	36

Table 11.3 (cont.)

		All %	10–14 %	Age 15–16 %	17 + %
School-leavers are unemployed	Agree	46	51	47	39
because older people have	Neither	28	29	31	26
taken all the jobs	Disagree	26	20	23	35
Young people don't get jobs	Agree	47	39	58	42
because they are not good at	Neither	25	37	18	22
'putting themselves over' in applications and interviews	Disagree	28	24	24	36
You can get a job if you are	Agree	50	54	54	37
well qualified	Neither	23	31	22	17
	Disagree	27	15	24	46
Young people who haven't got	Agree	31	38	34	16
work don't really want to work	Neither	26	31	26	20
or haven't looked hard enough	Disagree	43	31	40	64
If you are good looking and	Agree	28	30	26	30
have lots of confidence you'll	Neither	29	30	29	27
get a job	Disagree	43	40	45	43
To get a job, you need someone	Agree	36	35	35	37
with influence to 'put in a good	Neither	30	36	27	31
word' for you	Disagree	34	29	38	32
Going to the right school and	Agree	46	40	51	49
having the right contacts is a	Neither	28	34	26	22
big part of getting a job	Disagree	26	26	23	29

only 32 per cent believed that getting a job depends on *sheer* good luck.

There was some agreement that the influence of specific people on the job search was useful: 41 per cent believed those school-leavers who got jobs had people pulling strings for them, while 36 per cent believed that to get a job, you need someone with influence to put in a good word for you.

Young people tended to believe (61 per cent agreed) that unemployment is running so high because the jobs are not there, while 52 per cent believed the government is to blame for young people being out of work.

There were a number of dramatic age differences. Compared to younger respondents far fewer older respondents believed 'if they had better qualifications most of the unemployed would soon get jobs' (52 per cent vs. 25 per cent); 'Unemployed young people haven't tried hard enough and don't know how to sell themselves' (38 per cent vs. 25 per cent); 'If you miss out on getting work it is because you are not good enough' (30 per cent vs. 15 per cent); 'School-leavers are unemployed because older people have taken all the jobs' (51 per cent vs. 39 per cent); 'You can get a job if you are well qualified' (54 per cent vs. 37 per cent) and 'Young people who haven't got work don't really want to work or haven't looked hard enough' (38 per cent vs. 16 per cent).

On the other hand, older respondents agreed far more often than did younger respondents with various 'fatalistic' items such as 'Getting a job is mainly a matter of being in the right place at the right time' (69 per cent vs. 35 per cent); 'Unemployment is running so high because the jobs simply are not there' (65 per cent vs. 52 per cent) (see table 11.3).

One could agree that to some extent these results are an example of defensive attributions — that is, the idea that people explain success as due to effort and ability on their part but failure as due to luck, chance, or discrimination. Older respondents tended to be more fatalistic than younger people who felt getting a job more due to effort, ability, or talent. On the other hand, these results may be due to the fact that older respondents are much more familiar with the actual circumstances of getting a job today.

ATTITUDES TO SCHOOL

In all we put forward just over twenty-five items about our respondents' attitudes to school. The first statements concerned 'breaking the boundaries'. Students felt that they should be aware of their limitations (65 per cent) and that they should conform and not be too attention-seeking (56 per cent) though more younger respondents than older respondents agreed with this. Half thought it unfair for a particular student to show off and be the 'good pupil all the time' but this was less true of older than of younger respondents. Less than half in total, and more older than younger respondents, felt that one 'should not expect too much from school', though nearly one in three disagreed with this (see table 11.4).

We were also interested in the students' perceptions of the value of schooling. We asked ten questions about the general issue and found that, overall, the students tended to see schooling as a valuable experience. For instance, 63 per cent disagreed (particularly females

Table 11.4 Attitudes to school

%		All %	Male %	Female %	Age 10–14 %	15–16 %	17+ %
One should be aware of one's limitations in class if one wishes to be happy at school	Agree	65	64	66	64	66	66
	Neither	26	27	26	29	27	24
	Disagree	9	9	8	7	7	10
To get on at school it is best to behave like the other students in class and not draw the attention of the teacher to yourself too much	Agree	56	57	54	58	54	55
	Neither	23	24	23	27	21	23
	Disagree	21	19	23	15	25	22
It is not fair to the rest of the class for a student to try and be the 'good pupil' all the time	Agree	50	49	51	53	50	42
	Neither	24	24	24	25	23	26
	Disagree	26	27	25	22	27	32
You should not expect too much from school, for you would only be disappointed	Agree	45	49	41	43	43	50
	Neither	25	25	25	30	24	17
	Disagree	30	25	35	27	33	33
It really doesn't matter how well you do at school	Agree	22	26	18	22	18	27
	Neither	15	17	12	18	13	13
	Disagree	63	57	70	60	69	60
An educated person stands a better chance in life than an uneducated person	Agree	57	57	61	58	60	58
	Neither	20	23	17	26	17	19
	Disagree	23	20	22	16	23	23
People like me find it difficult to get good jobs no matter how much education we have	Agree	43	43	43	41	44	42
	Neither	30	32	29	37	28	28
	Disagree	27	25	28	22	28	30
Employers pay a lot of attention to school reports and examination results	Agree	64	64	72	59	75	70
	Neither	20	22	17	29	17	14
	Disagree	16	14	11	12	8	16
It is wise to think about next year's schoolwork rather than concentrate on what you're doing now	Agree	27	32	22	23	31	26
	Neither	30	31	28	31	29	28
	Disagree	43	37	50	46	40	46
A lot of schooling is necessary to avoid a dead-end job	Agree	59	51	49	46	54	48
	Neither	29	28	29	34	26	23
	Disagree	22	21	22	20	20	29
Failure in examinations ruins a person's chances in life	Agree	36	38	35	41	37	26
	Neither	22	24	21	28	22	18
	Disagree	42	38	44	31	41	56
Some people require education for their jobs but for most of us it is a waste of time	Agree	29	29	29	26	32	26
	Neither	27	30	25	33	26	25
	Disagree	44	41	46	41	42	49
School helps you become independent	Agree	64	61	67	69	60	56
	Neither	18	19	17	19	19	16
	Disagree	18	21	16	12	21	28

167

Table 11.4 (cont.)

		All %	Male %	Female %	Age 10–14 %	15–16 %	17 + %
School teaches about	Agree	62	63	61	68	64	53
different sorts of careers	Neither	20	19	21	24	20	15
	Disagree	18	18	18	8	16	33
I get bored and fed up with	Agree	39	41	37	41	47	28
school and do not really	Neither	27	28	25	28	25	26
enjoy anything connected	Disagree	34	31	38	31	28	46
with it							
Examinations are the only	Agree	35	38	33	44	32	29
fair test of a student's	Neither	22	20	24	34	15	17
knowledge	Disagree	43	42	43	22	53	54
Participation in classroom	Agree	70	71	68	60	70	78
discussions is more valuable	Neither	22	20	25	30	20	18
than teachers explaining	Disagree	8	9	7	10	10	4
everything							
Technical and academic	Agree	72	74	71	59	78	82
subjects should be offered	Neither	21	19	24	32	18	13
in the same school	Disagree	7	7	5	9	4	5
We should be able to	Agree	64	61	68	59	62	71
undertake projects useful to	Neither	27	28	26	31	29	21
the community as part of	Disagree	9	11	6	10	9	8
our school work							
I would be learning	Agree	75	75	76	69	81	73
better if classes were more	Neither	19	19	18	22	15	19
interesting	Disagree	6	6	6	9	4	8
It should be possible to	Agree	47	49	46	49	47	50
work and attend a normal	Neither	25	25	26	29	25	21
school part-time (2 days a	Disagree	28	26	28	22	28	29
week)							
Most of the subjects I	Agree	55	50	59	59	52	62
take are interesting	Neither	22	25	18	21	21	25
	Disagree	23	25	23	20	27	13
The most important thing	Agree	57	56	58	55	60	57
about school is making	Neither	25	29	23	25	26	29
friends	Disagree	18	15	19	20	14	14
To get on at school	Agree	42	46	37	43	39	47
you must put yourself first	Neither	33	30	36	36	34	27
	Disagree	25	24	27	21	27	26
Students should not expect	Agree	41	49	33	44	39	44
teachers to like them	Neither	30	28	33	33	30	25
	Disagree	29	23	34	23	31	31
Teachers are good at	Agree	34	39	31	40	30	34
getting their ideas across	Neither	34	30	35	30	33	32
in the classroom	Disagree	32	31	34	30	37	34

compared to males) that it doesn't really matter how well you do at school. Similarly, 44 per cent disagreed (again more females than males) that education is mostly a waste of time. On the other hand, nearly two-thirds believed that school teaches about different sorts of careers (62 per cent), helps to make you become independent (64 per cent), and that employers pay close attention to examination results (74 per cent). More than half also believed that an educated person stands a better chance in life than an uneducated person (57 per cent) and that schooling helps to avoid dead-end jobs (50 per cent). But more disagreed with the idea that failure in examinations ruins a person's chance in life (42 per cent vs. 36 per cent) and that it is wise to think about next year's school work rather than concentrate on the present.

There were some noticeable sex and age differences with respect to these questions. Overall, females tended to value schooling more than males. For instance, 70 per cent of females compared to 57 per cent of males disagreed with the statement that 'it really doesn't matter how well you do at school', while 71 per cent of females agreed, compared to 57 per cent of males, that an educated person stands a better chance in life.

We were also interested in the attitudes of our respondents to the school curriculum and innovation. Three questions showed nearly three-quarters of the sample agreeing, each with dramatic age differences. In all, 70 per cent agreed that participation in class is more valuable than teachers explaining everything (78 per cent older, 60 per cent younger); 72 per cent agreed that technical and academic subjects should be taught in the same school (82 per cent older, 59 per cent younger); and 75 per cent agreed that they would learn better if the classes were more interesting (73 per cent vs. 69 per cent). The only item that elicited more disagreement than agreement, particularly among older compared to younger respondents (58 per cent vs. 22 per cent), was that examinations are the only fair test of a student's knowledge.

About two-thirds (64 per cent) agreed that school-children should undertake, in school, projects useful to the community and females agreed with this more than males. Females also agreed more than males (59 per cent vs. 50 per cent) that most of the subjects they take are interesting though they agreed less often than did males (37 per cent vs. 46 per cent) that to get on at school you must put yourself first.

Finally, we asked two questions about teachers. Almost equal numbers believed and did not believe that teachers are good at getting their ideas across in the classroom, but slightly more agreed than disagreed (41 per cent vs. 29 per cent) that students should not expect teachers to like them. While there were no significant age differences on these questions, there were significant sex differences — females agreed with them less than males did.

CONCLUDING REMARKS

In this chapter we were concerned with young people's attitudes to work, jobs, unemployment, and school. Most of the young people were at school, a number were about to leave and seek work, while some were unemployed and others at work. We were not able to separate these groups but chose quite simply to look at the general attitudes of the sample as a whole.

Our sample expected both inflation and unemployment to go up during the following year. They believed, however, that the government's priority should be to reduce unemployment rather than inflation. They did not expect much difference in Britain's overall economic performance, but more felt optimistic than pessimistic about it. Retrospectively it is probably true to say that prices did go up a little in the period as did unemployment, though the official figures showed only a small increase.

The results from questions on work ethic showed that young Britons were neither work-shy nor workaholic. Most (nearly two-thirds) felt that hard work made someone a better person and nearly a half thought that one could ascertain a person's worth through their job. They did believe in relaxation after work, however, and that work was a means to an end rather than an end in itself. To this extent one might argue that young people have a fairly healthy attitude to work.

Like adults already at work, our youth sample tended not to believe that salaries and working hours were the most important features of a job. They rated security most highly which no doubt reflects the current state of unemployment. But the intrinsic nature of the job as well as pleasant working conditions and colleagues were considered very important too.

To some extent, whether a person gets the sort of job he or she desires is dependent not only on their ability, skills, and qualifications, but also on how they go about getting a job. We were interested in the various beliefs of young people with respect to job search. By and large, they did not think that powerful or influential people were very useful for getting a job. But a fairly large number of older children tended to think there was an element of luck in getting a job. Certainly, older respondents tended to deny, more than did younger respondents, that people's lack of jobs implied that they did not put effort into the job search, rather than that the jobs simply did not exist.

The response to the attitudes to school statements did not reveal any major surprises. Our respondents tended to value schooling and place emphasis on the benefits of schooling. Yet they did tend to wish their lessons to be more interesting, relevant to the community, and to mix technical and academic subjects. Certainly, they did not tend to blame teachers for all their difficulties and thought that schooling is necessary in the development of a number of important skills.

Whereas some topics have tended to show up a number of sex differences, particularly those subject scores concerned with political and social affairs, much more prevalent here were age differences. This is perhaps to be expected because the youngest group in our sample were mainly at the beginning of their secondary schooling, while the older group were at the end of or, in some cases, had finished with their schooling and were actually in the labour market. It is not surprising then that there were often dramatic differences in percep- tions of the most desirable features of a job, how to get a job, or the value of school.

Chapter Twelve

HOME ENTERTAINMENT MEDIA

Young people today have more spare time on their hands, more money to spend, and a greater variety of things on which to spend it than at any time in the past. There is an unprecedented range of leisure pursuits within their grasp and a growing array of home entertainment media. Both inside the home and outside it, adolescents have a variety of choice with regard to personal amusement (and edification) which surpasses anything available to any previous 'young generation'. Since television, video, sound systems, personal computers, and other related items and gadgets play such a prominent role in the lives of young people today, we felt that how they are used and what gratifications they bring are important areas of enquiry. In this chapter we explore the hobbies and leisure activities and use of home-based electronic entertainment media by our young sample.

TELEVISION VIEWING

Television is practically a universal feature of households in Britain today. In all, 98 per cent of homes in the country possess at least one television set. Indeed, the norm these days is to have more than one set and the trend towards multiple set ownership has continued steadily upwards during the 1980s (IBA 1987). Television has, however, expanded in all sorts of ways. The location of television sets within the house, for instance, has changed. Most people have a set in the main living room, while the next most popular location is a bedroom (IBA 1987).

Nearly everyone watches television at least sometimes. As a device used simply to receive off-air broadcasts, the average television set is used for about five hours a day. These days, however, the basic set can be enhanced in a variety of ways as a range of accessories — video recorders, video disc player, teletext and viewdata services, video games, and home computers — have come on to the market. There are also alternative sources of programming provided by cable and satellite television services. All these developments have resulted in significant changes to the way television is used in the home. A recent survey indicated that nearly six out of ten people (57 per cent) claimed to have at least one extra feature among a list of alternatives given (IBA 1987).

The most widespread accessory is the video recorder, with more than four out of ten viewers having one. Nearly one in five viewers have acquired teletext television receivers, while somewhat more have home computers. One in ten viewers claim to have video games and there also appears to be the start of growth of domestic video cameras. All of these features tend to be more commonplace in households with children and young people (IBA 1987).

Television can serve different functions for different people. One of the most important services provided by television in the opinions of many viewers is its daily news (BBC 1977). On average, around two out of three people in modern, industrialized societies claim that television is their main source of national and international news (IBA 1987; Roper Organization 1983). In Britain, there has been a continuing trend towards television becoming *the* source of world news, leaving other sources such as radio and newspapers further behind. Despite the near universality of television, however, together with the variety of new enhancements which add to its attractiveness, people still listen to radio and read newspapers on a wide scale. In 1986, around eight out of ten adults were found to report listening to radio nowadays. Most people have access to at least one radio set in the home, and multiple radio set ownership, as with multiple television set ownership, is becoming more prevalent (IBA 1987).

In this chapter we examine young people's use of various sources of home entertainment. We asked our youth sample about their television-viewing, radio-listening, and newspaper-reading habits. We also investigated their use of other sources of amusement in the home, particularly those relating to the new television-linked accessories.

More than eight out of ten (83 per cent) of our youth sample claimed to watch television 'at least once every day', with most of the remainder (16 per cent) claiming to watch at least 'once a week'. Only a negligible proportion (less than 1 per cent) said that they never watched television.

Some differences in claimed frequency of watching television were found in connection with the age of respondents. Those in their late teens (72 per cent) were less likely than either 15–16s (86 per cent) or 10–14s (92 per cent) to say that they watched television every day.

Watching the news on television was commonplace among young people. Whether this was done out of preference for this type of programme and the need to keep up with what is happening in the world, or whether the news was seen simply because of watching a lot of television *per se* is not something we were able to disentangle. More than half our youth respondents (51 per cent) claimed to watch the news broadcast on television every day, while a further four out of ten (43 per cent) watched the news at least once a week. Males (53 per cent) were more likely than females (48 per cent) to say they watched television news broadcasts every day.

PERCEIVED REALISM OF TELEVISION

To what extent do young people perceive television as showing things in a realistic light? We asked our youth sample to say how often they thought that television news and television drama programmes present things like they are in real life. The news was perceived to be realistic more often than drama. Nine per cent perceived the news always to be true to life, compared with just 2 per cent who believed the same of drama. More than half (55 per cent) thought that the news is realistic 'quite often', compared with one in three (34 per cent) who thought that this was the case with drama. Just under one in three (57 per cent) thought that the news was realistic 'only sometimes' compared with more than half who said this with respect to drama. Relatively few believed that either the news (20 per cent) or drama (7 per cent) always showed things in a realistic manner.

The youngest respondents (10–14s) (13 per cent) were more likely than 15–16s (8 per cent) or those aged 17 + (5 per cent) to believe that television news 'always' shows things like they are in real life. With respect to television drama, 3 per cent or fewer across age groups thought that it is always true to life. However, 38 per cent of 10–14s thought that drama can quite often be realistic compared with 35 per cent of 15–16-year-olds and 29 per cent of those aged 17 and over.

TIMES OF WATCHING TELEVISION

In the past few years, the hours over which television programmes are broadcast have expanded considerably. New early morning television services began on two television channels in 1983, starting at around 6.30 a.m. More recently, daytime programming has been introduced to link up breakfast television with afternoon transmissions and some television companies have begun to experiment with late-night and round-the-clock programming. We wished to find out the extent to which young people either began their viewing early in the day or stayed up very late to watch television's offerings.

Over one in three (37 per cent) said they never watched breakfast television, while fewer than one in twenty (4 per cent) claimed never to watch late at night. Regular viewing after 10.30 p.m. was far more common among our youth sample than was early morning viewing. More than eight out of ten (83 per cent) claimed to watch until late at least two or three times a week, which was about double the proportions who claimed to watch television early in the day at least that often (43 per cent).

Table 12.1 Frequency of watching late-night television as a function of sex, age, and social class

	Male %	Female %	10–14 %	15–16 %	17 + %	ABC1 %	C2 %	DE %
Every day	40	25	24	38	37	27	35	36
4–5 times a week	24	20	26	23	22	20	23	23
2–3 times a week	23	32	24	25	24	30	26	28
Once a week	5	10	10	7	6	10	7	6
Less than once a week	5	9	9	5	8	9	6	5
Never	2	5	6	2	3	4	3	2

Males (21 per cent) and females (22 per cent) differed hardly at all in their claims about watching breakfast television. There were, however, differences associated with the age of respondents. The 10–14s were far more likely than the 15–16s (22 per cent) or the 17 + s (11 per cent) to say they watched breakfast television every day.

There were differences in reported frequency of watching late-night television associated with the sex, age, and class of respondents. Males were more likely than females to be frequent late-night viewers. Frequency of staying up late to watch television was also more common among older rather than younger respondents and among working-class compared with middle-class respondents (table 12.1). Even so, younger and middle-class respondents were still highly likely to watch until late at least two or three times a week. Among 10–14-year-olds (55 per cent), however, late night viewing seemed to be reserved for the weekends while few (7 per cent) claimed to stay up late to watch television mainly during the week. Four out of ten 10–14s (38 per cent) watched both at weekends and during weekdays, compared with more than half the 15–16s (53 per cent) and 17 + s (56 per cent) who made the same claim.

LISTENING TO RADIO

Despite the claimed high frequency of watching television among most of our respondents, there was no indication that radio listening had suffered in consequence. Half (50 per cent) claimed to listen to the radio every day, while fewer than one in twenty (4 per cent) said they never listened. Fourteen per cent said they listened four to five times a week and 16 per cent two to three times a week. Females (58 per cent) were more avid radio users than males (42 per cent)

Just over one in four (27 per cent) said that they listened to the news on radio every day, while a further 14 per cent said they listened to it at least four to five times a week and 17 per cent two or three times a week. One in five (20 per cent) said they never listened to radio news. Age was an important factor here. Frequent listening to radio news broadcasts increased with age. Four out of ten (40 per cent) of 17 + -year-olds listened every day compared to 25 per cent of 15–16-year-olds and 18 per cent of 10–14-year-olds.

NEWSPAPER READING

Nearly half our respondents (46 per cent) claimed to read a daily morning newspaper, while round just one in ten (11 per cent) said that they never did. Newspaper reading increased with age and was more likely to be a popular habit among respondents from a working-class background. More than half those aged 15 years and over (51 per cent) compared with less than four in ten (32 per cent) younger respondents claimed to read a paper everyday. Four in ten (40 per cent) middle-class respondents claimed to read a paper every day against more than half (50 per cent) of the working-class adolescents.

Those who said they read daily morning newspapers were asked to say which one(s) they normally read. Readership of the tabloids was much more widespread than that of broadsheets. More than four out of ten claimed to read the *Sun*. The next most popularly read daily newspaper was the *Daily Mirror*. More than one in four also said they read a local daily newspaper (see table 12.2)

Table 12.2 Name of newspaper normally read

	All %
The Sun	43
Daily Mirror/Record	29
Daily Mail	15
Daily Star	13
Daily Express	13
The Times	7
Daily Telegraph	6
The Guardian	5
Financial Times	1
Local daily newspaper	27

We also asked our respondents about their reading of Sunday newspapers. Nearly nine out of ten (86 per cent) claimed to read a Sunday newspaper at least sometimes. Nearly two-thirds (64 per cent) said they read one every week. The extent to which our respondents reported reading Sunday newspapers increased with age. Among 10–14s, 59 per cent claimed to read a Sunday paper every week compared with 61 per cent of 15–16s and 17 + s.

Table 12.3 Name of Sunday newspaper normally read

	All %
Sunday Mirror	32
News of the World	32
Sunday People	22
Mail on Sunday	15
Sunday Express	14
Sunday Times	9
The Observer	6
Sunday Telegraph	4

Once again, we asked those respondents who read a Sunday newspaper at all to indicate which one(s) they read. Two newspapers emerged as the most popular by some distance. Both the *Sunday Mirror* and the *News of the World* were reportedly read by around one in three Sunday newspaper readers. Least popularly read among our youth sample were those papers normally considered to occupy the 'serious' end of the market — *Sunday Telegraph, Observer*, and *Sunday Times* (see table 12.3).

ACCESS TO AND USE OF HOME ENTERTAINMENT MEDIA

We began by looking at the range of home entertainment young people had available to them and what use they made of these media. Responses revealed widespread access to a range of media and media attachments or gadgets. More than nine out of ten respondents claimed to have the use of an audio-tape or cassette player (94 per cent) and a record player (93 per cent) where they lived. Nearly six out of ten (59 per cent) said they had the use of a video cassette recorder. This figure is higher than the national average (44 per cent), but compares favourably with the figure for family households with children (58 per cent) (IBA 1987). Nearly half (48 per cent) claimed to have a home computer. The use of a teletext receiver (for Oracle or Ceefax) was less commonplace, but the one in three (36 per cent) who claimed to have one is double the national average (IBA 1987).

Table 12.4 Access to and use of home entertainment media

	All %	Male %	Female %
Do you have the use of it where you live?			
Audio, tape or cassette player	94	93	95
Record (disc) player, gramophone	93	93	91
Video cassette recorder	59	63	54
Remote control TV switch	53	56	50
Home computer	48	51	43
Oracle and Ceefax on the TV	34	37	32
How many of the following items have you got that you do use from time to time? (Those who say they have use of any)			
Audio discs/records	91	90	92
Audio cassettes recorded at home	92	92	93
Audio cassettes factory recorded	80	81	80
Video cassettes on which you tape programmes	59	62	55
Recorded video cassettes which you will not wipe off	44	46	43

Just as there was widespread use of audio-cassette and record players, so too, there was extensive claimed use of audio-discs/records (91 per cent). Self-recorded audio-cassettes (92 per cent) were more widespread than factory recorded cassettes (80 per cent), and self-recorded *video* cassettes were used more widely (59 per cent) than pre-recorded videos (44 per cent) (table 12.4).

USE OF COMPUTERS AT HOME

Among the range of accessory items which have expanded the use of the television set during the 1980s, one of the most prominent developments has been the home computer. Recent national survey results indicate that around one in five adults claim to have a home computer, and more than one in three adults with children say they have one (IBA 1987). About half those proportions in each group say they have video games at home, too.

We asked our young respondents about their use of computers and video games at home, and found far more extensive claims in each instance among this particular age group. More than four out of ten (43 per cent) claimed to have either a home computer or a video game set at home while nine out of ten (90 per cent) said they had never used a computer. Among those who said they had a computer at home, nearly half (48 per cent) claimed to use it at least a few times a week. Males were more likely than females to have a video game at home (48 per cent versus 36 per cent) or a home computer (49 per cent versus 38 per cent). Among those who claimed to have a computer at home, males (65 per cent) were more likely than females (55 per cent) to say they used it at least once a week.

USE OF COMPUTERS AT SCHOOL

Even more young people who do not have a computer available to them at home may have some experience in computing through school. One national survey of children's media use recently found that most children said they had a computer at school (Gunter and Greenberg 1986). Those findings are confirmed here. More than nine out of ten respondents (93 per cent) said that their school had a computer which students could use and 7 per cent said they did not. Usage of the school computer was not as frequent as usage of a personal computer at home, presumably because it had to be shared with many others. Ten per cent said they used it every day, 13 per cent a few times a week, 16 per cent about once a week, 32 per cent once or twice a month and 30 per cent said they never used one. Nine per cent said they were not allowed to use it. Nearly six out of ten (58 per cent) said they had had a class in computers while four in ten (42 per cent) said they had not.

BELIEFS ABOUT COMPUTERS

In addition to finding out about access to and use of computers, we attempted to find out what young people think about computers. In what ways can they benefit society? Are some people more suited to use them than others? From an initial set of four statements to each of which true or false responses were requested, it emerged that young people predominantly believe that computers are improving our quality of life (72 per cent true, 28 per cent false), but that they will increase unemployment (63 per cent true, 32 per cent false). Nevertheless, knowing how to use a computer can help you to find a job (62 per cent true, 38 per cent false). Finally, both boys and girls should be able to use a computer (82 per cent rejected the proposition that it is easier for boys than for girls to learn to use a computer while 18 per cent accepted it).

Opinions differed between the sexes. Males (79 per cent) were more likely than females (65 per cent) to believe that computers can improve the quality of life; that knowing how to use them can help you find a job (67 per cent versus 58 per cent); and that boys can learn how to use them more easily than girls (22 per cent versus 13 per cent).

The respondents agreed that everyone should be taught to use a computer (65 per cent) and that it is just as important for girls to learn to use them as it is for boys (82 per cent). Computers were seen as being likely to reduce the differences between the jobs done by men and women (62 per cent). Some confirmation of responses given to an earlier statement emerged, as over half of respondents (55 per cent) disagreed that men are better at programming computers than women, with less than one in five agreeing with this (18 per cent). There was a substantial difference between males and females on this opinion, however. Females (70 per cent) were much more likely to disagree with it than were males (42 per cent).

Despite certain advantages and benefits of computers, young people do not necessarily accept them. Few respondents (15 per cent) felt that having more and more things done by machines is a good thing. More (28 per cent) felt it is a bad thing, while many (57 per cent) felt it would be a bit of both. Overall, males (21 per cent) tended more often to see it as better than did females (9 per cent).

INTERESTS AND HOBBIES

Finally, we gave our respondents a list of eighty-six interests and hobbies and asked them to indicate how interested they were in each one along a four-point scale ('not at all', 'not very', 'fairly', or 'extremely interested'). These activities were broken down into nine categories:

1. interests in different sports
2. interests in outdoor pursuits
3. interests in indoor games
4. interests in practical hobbies
5. interests in motoring
6. interests in home-based leisure pursuits
7. interests in out-of-home leisure pursuits
8. interests in domestic activities
9. interests in social/community organizations

INTERESTS IN DIFFERENT SPORTS

Respondents were provided with a list of twenty-three different sports and asked to indicate their degree of interest in each one. The results presented in table 12.5 show the summed percentages over those who said they found each sport 'fairly' or 'extremely' interesting. The most popular sports among our sample of adolescents were swimming, billiards/pool, tennis, table tennis, and ice-skating. In each case more than half said they found them at least 'fairly interesting'. The least popular sports were golf, bowling, and horse racing, for each of which one in five or fewer respondents indicated some interest. Of course, it ought to be borne in mind when interpreting these results that respondents were simply indicating their personal degree of interest in a sport, and not whether they actually played it. It is possible that among those sports that are of most interest are ones which respondents have also played themselves. On the other hand, interest may signify

Table 12.5 Interests in different sports

	All %	Male %	Female %
Swimming	66	62	70
Billiards/pool	63	77	48
Tennis	56	49	62
Table tennis	54	46	51
Ice-skating	53	38	68
Soccer	47	64	30
Basketball	43	45	40
Snow skiing	42	41	42
Water skiing	41	42	39
Volleyball	37	34	39
Jogging	35	35	35
Boating	35	38	31
Squash	35	38	32
Auto racing	31	50	11
Judo/karate	30	33	27
Hockey	29	21	37
Boxing	27	39	14
Baseball	27	32	22
Fishing	24	36	12
Hunting	23	32	13
Horse racing	20	17	23
Bowling	17	22	12
Golf	16	21	11

Note: Percentages are those who claimed to find each sport 'fairly' or 'extremely' interesting.

no more than that they enjoy watching these sports being played, either live or on television.

There were a number of substantial sex differences in stated sports interests. Males were much more likely than females to be interested in auto-racing, billiards/pool, soccer, boxing, and fishing. Females were more interested than males in ice-skating, tennis, and hockey.

INTERESTS IN OUTDOOR PURSUITS

We looked at interests in four outdoor pursuits. As table 12.6 reveals, around six out of ten respondents indicated an interest in travel and sight-seeing and in camping. Both males and females expressed an interest in these activities. Fewer were keen on either back-packing or hiking.

Table 12.6 Interests in outdoor pursuits

	All %	Male %	Female %
Travel/sight-seeing	60	55	65
Camping	58	57	58
Hiking	28	31	24
Back-packing	17	23	10

INTERESTS IN INDOOR GAMES

Indoor games were not widely of interest. Card playing and board games such as backgammon, scrabble, or monopoly were found to be interesting by just under half our respondents. Between one in four and one in three were interested in chess or draughts, party games, or crossword and jigsaw puzzles (see table 12.7). Females were more likely than males to be interested in the latter two while males were more likely to opt for chess or draughts.

Table 12.7 Interests in indoor games

	All %	Male %	Female %
Card playing	47	49	44
Board games (backgammon, scrabble, monopoly)	45	45	44
Crossword/jigsaw puzzles	31	26	36
Party games	29	24	34
Chess/draughts	26	31	20

INTERESTS IN PRACTICAL HOBBIES

These were even less widely popular than indoor games. Photography and playing a musical instrument were most likely to be found interesting, endorsed by more than one in three respondents. Painting and needlework were interesting for around one in four, more predominantly among females than among males, however. Fewer than one in five indicated an interest in any other practical hobbies, though females did reveal a much wider interest in ceramics and pottery than did males (see table 12.8).

Table 12.8 Interests in practical hobbies

	All %	Male %	Female %
Photography	39	36	42
Playing a musical instrument	34	32	36
Painting	26	21	30
Needlework	25	9	41
Model building	18	28	8
Ceramics/pottery	17	11	23
Coin/stamp collecting	12	15	9
Sculpture	10	6	13

INTERESTS IN MOTORING

A majority of respondents were interested in driving and just under half were also interested in motor cycles. Auto repair was of less interest, particularly among females. Indeed, females were less interested generally in anything connected with motoring than were males (table 12.9).

Table 12.9 Interests in motoring

	All %	Male %	Female %
Driving/motoring	64	72	55
Motor cycles	47	57	36
Auto repair	24	38	10

INTERESTS IN HOME-BASED LEISURE PURSUITS

These included television, video, radio, reading, listening to music, and new electronic gadgetry and equipment. Television and watching video films were easily the most popular among both males and females, with video being somewhat more widely liked by males. Other popular leisure activities in the home included listening to radio and popular music. Reading, too, was endorsed by half the respondents, though much more so by females than by males. Nearly four out of ten indicated an interest in home computers. Poetry and classical music were least likely to be found interesting by the adolescents we questioned (see table 12.10);

Table 12.10 Interests in home-based leisure activities

	All %	Male %	Female %
Television	83	83	82
Watching video films	77	82	72
Radio	70	70	69
Popular music	60	62	58
Reading	51	41	60
Home computer	39	42	35
Literature	34	27	40
CB radio	22	24	19
Classical music	20	17	22
Poetry	18	12	24

INTERESTS IN OUT-OF-HOME LEISURE PURSUITS

Going to the cinema remains very popular with young people, with around three out of four indicating here that they find movies interesting. Despite the popularity of a range of home-based activities, most respondents nevertheless indicated that visiting friends was important to them. Other widely enjoyed leisure activities included dancing, eating out, and amusement arcades. Females especially indicated a strong interest in dancing and eating out (see table 12.11).

Table 12.11 Interests in out-of-home leisure pursuits

	All %	Male %	Female %
Movies (cinema)	76	71	80
Visiting friends	74	70	78
Dancing	60	50	70
Amusement arcades	53	56	50
Dining out	53	42	63
Live theatre	33	22	43
Ballet	10	7	13
Opera	8	7	8

INTERESTS IN DOMESTIC ACTIVITIES

With the exception of entertainment at home, domestic activities generally were of little interest to most of our young people. Another departure from this pattern was a fairly widespread interest in cooking and preparing meals among females. Household cleaning, tending to indoor plants, and gardening were particularly unpopular (table 12.12).

Table 12.12 Interests in domestic activities

	All %	Male %	Female %
Entertaining at home	65	64	65
Meal preparation	36	25	46
Interior decorating	25	23	26
Gourmet cooking	25	19	30
Maintenance/repairs of home	22	34	19
Gardening	19	20	18
Household management	19	15	22
Indoor plants	17	13	20
House cleaning	15	10	20

INTERESTS IN SOCIAL/COMMUNITY ORGANIZATIONS

The great majority of respondents were interested in their youth clubs, but little else. One in three said they were interested in community functions, while fewer than one in four were interested in child-related or local cultural activities. In general, females were more likely than males to indicate any interest in social and community organizations (see table 12:13).

Table 12.13 Interests in social and community organizations

	All %	Male %	Female %
Youth clubs	81	77	85
Community/social functions	34	28	39
Child-related activities (PTA, Scouts, etc.)	23	19	27
Local cultural activities	23	19	26
Religious organizations' activities	15	11	19

CONCLUDING REMARKS

In this chapter we have examined the use of various home entertainment media by our youth sample. It was abundantly clear that young people today have a large number and variety of forms of amusement available to them. It came as no surprise to find that television watching was almost universal, and that daily viewing was characteristic of the great majority of respondents. Viewing was somewhat less prominent among older teenagers, though even among these a substantial majority claimed to watch every day.

Our young people often watched the news, though whether this was motivated by special interest or occurred simply because they watched a lot of television in general was not distinguished. News was widely perceived to be realistic and true to life in its depiction of events, while drama was seen in this light by fewer respondents. The news was not thought invariably to reflect reality, however, while drama was perceived on occasions to do so.

Television broadcast hours have expanded as a result of new early morning and daytime programmes as well as the extension of programmes late into the night. Among our sample, both types of programmes were watched by substantial proportions of our young people, with late-night viewing, especially at weekends, being most popular.

Despite the time devoted to watching television, most respondents were also regular radio listeners and readers of newspapers. In effect then, most young people today would seem to be regular users of many different media, between which they share their time.

In addition to television, radio, and newspapers, most also claimed to have access to and to use audio- and tape-players, video-recorders, and record-players. Home computers and teletext television services were also widely used. The vast majority had used a computer at home and at school. And more than half of those who said they had a computer at home claimed to use it at least once a week. Regarding computers, our adolescent and youth respondents believed that they improved the quality of life. There was widespread belief that everyone should know how to use computers, and that boys are no better than girls in acquiring this ability. Further beliefs were that computer literacy can help you to find a job, but the growth of computers would result in increased unemployment as machines take over many of the jobs formerly done by people.

The findings for media availability and use tally with earlier research data from among children in Britain up to age 12, which revealed that most youngsters live in media-rich home environments where they learn to share out their leisure time between many different technologically-based forms of entertainment, with each one providing a particular gratification (Gunter and Greenberg 1986).

The young people in this survey revealed that they had a fairly wide spread of interests which were related to hobbies and leisure activities both inside and outside the home. The most popular out-of-home activities were sports and outdoor pursuits such as travel and camping. Indoors, our young people were interested mostly in television and video, with evidence that listening to the radio and reading were still enjoyed by many. There is some indication that practical hobbies and board games are of interest to some young people, but also that new electronic gadgetry and equipment such as home computers are becoming increasingly prominent. It is difficult, however, always to disentangle what is meant by interest in this context. In the case of some interests, we may be measuring not only the fact that something is liked but also that it is a pursuit or hobby which respondents actively pursue. In other cases, their stated interest may reveal simply that they like to watch it or read about it, but do not actually practise, play, or perform it themselves. Whatever is being measured (and it is likely that both of these things are indicated here), it does seem that young people today have a great variety and choice of hobbies and activities with which to fill their leisure time. Finding the time to do or follow all the things they claim to be interested in is likely to become increasingly difficult.

Chapter Thirteen

THE CHANGING PRIORITIES AND CONCERNS OF ADOLESCENTS

This book has concerned the anatomy of British adolescents' attitudes, beliefs, behaviours, and values in the 1980s. The foregoing chapters concern the social attitudes of a nationwide sample of British adolescents who were questioned in 1985 (International Youth Year) and 1986. The questionnaire covered a very wide range of topics from sex to politics, religion to leisure. In our choice of topics we hoped to look at the major interests and priorities of young people in connection with what confronts them in their home, their school, or workplace, and their local community and society at large.

It is from the monitoring and understanding of *trends* in young people's knowledge, beliefs, and values that one can begin to learn what is happening in society. We hope that the foregoing chapters give a fair and accurate picture of the expectations, interests, priorities, and concerns of young people which provide an insight into the current state of British adolescence. Many of these beliefs and behaviours are likely to change and others to remain the same. Economic, political, and social forces over the remaining years of this century are likely to lead to various changes in people's work, social relationships, and life-style. External changes may well have an important effect on adolescents' beliefs and behaviours will change. For instance, there is little to suggest that political attitudes or knowledge will increase but it is quite probable that employment, sex role, and leisure attitudes change quite considerably over a generation.

It would, however, be incorrect to assume that social, economic, and political forces are the only or major factors in *shaping* young people's perceptions. Not only are there other important factors such as the school and the family, but just as external forces change attitudes so too attitudes, as expressed through votes, purchases, and affiliations, shape external forces. Young people have fairly considerable purchasing power which can have dramatic effects on the range, type, and quality of product that manufacturers provide to fulfil a need. Many young people of 18 years and older are able to vote in local and national elections and, hence, their hopes and fears may play an important role in political affairs. The desire of young people for further education, different types of media, local amenities, and so on can cause substantial changes in the way communities are organized.

Young people, then, change, and are changed by, the society in which they live. To understand the form and nature of these changes we need to know what young people do, think about, and value in their lives. What future do they want and how do they set about trying to attain it? How do they react to the adult roles they have to take on? What is their perception of how far they are allowed to reject adult behaviour patterns? What is the awareness of the industrial, social, and legal practices that prevent them from doing what they want to do?

In this final chapter we hope to discuss three things: first, some of the broad *themes* that could be detected in this morass of findings; second, some *comparative* issues of sex, age, and class; and, third, a few *methodological* points.

THEMATIC ISSUES

There are, of course, both positive and negative perspectives on adolescence. From a positive perspective, adolescents are seen to demonstrate *youthful idealism*, being concerned with crime, drug abuse, nuclear disarmament, materialism, pollution and the environment, and the plight of the Third World. Very often young people show a serious concern for the underdog and will give generously and do voluntary work to help the poor and those from developing countries. Frequently, but more often in times of affluence and expansion, they adopt anti-materialist philosophies and reject what they perceive to be the insincere, corrupt, or superficial values of adults. To some extent these features were discernible in this study. Our respondents were concerned about crime levels, the plight of developing countries, the environment, and social issues.

Negative stereotypes concerning adolescence include the idea that young people are pampered and spoiled, irresponsible, hedonistic, immoral, cynical, and rebellious. The sorts of questions that were asked in this study did not allow much opportunity to test the truthfulness of these stereotypes. Rather we concentrated on social, familial, moral, educational, and vocational questions. From these a number of themes seemed to emerge.

Optimism vs. pessimism

Were young people basically optimistic about the future of their world or, uncharacteristically for youth, pessimistic? The results tended to support both extremes. Young people in our survey tended to be pessimistic about work and unemployment, crime and law enforcement, health matters, and nuclear disarmament, but optimistic about the performance of certain institututions and governmental processes, the role of Britain in Europe, the role of men and women, and the effects of new technology.

Naive vs. sophisticated

Were the young people naive and simplistic in their views or sophisticated in their understanding of the complex way in which society operates? Again, the answer is both. Some questions that referred to how things are, rather than how they should be, did show the sample to be somewhat naive as compared to how adults responded. This seemed particularly to be the case with respect to political, governmental, and international issues. On the other hand, respondents clearly demonstrated their interest in, commitment to, and understanding of issues relating to health, the environment, school, and new technology.

Alienated vs. committed

To what extent do young people appear to be alienated from or committed to society and all its institutions? Much has been written about alienated youth with their feelings of powerlessness, normlessness, hopelessness, and estrangement. Certainly the results from this study did not support the idea that young people are alienated on a large scale. On the contrary, and especially with issues that naturally are close to their personal experience like schooling and new technology, young people appeared to be generally committed to the efficient functioning of the roles and institutions currently existing in society. That is not to say that there was no evidence of alienation but rather that it was focused on specific issues.

Revolutionary vs. reactionary

To what extent are young people revolutionary in their attitudes, beliefs, and values about their society, or reactionary, wishing for a return to a supposed 'idyllic' earlier period? Whereas to many of the above questions the answer has been both, the answer to this question is more probably neither. Young people seem to be involved with both 'youth culture and adult culture', seeking neither to subvert the latter nor to replace it with the former. This is not to say that they are against change, but rather that the change they appear to favour is moderate and limited.

There may well be other themes that can be perceived in the foregoing pages. Furthermore, readers may perceive various 'isms' like racism and sexism. But the evidence is not strong for the existence of any one strongly held creed. For example, the young white people we surveyed tended to be largely accepting of ethnic minorities. We observed a highly promising trend towards wanting equality of opportunity for other races on a wide social and occupational scale. However, there remained an undercurrent of suspicion and wariness about closer ties with other races. It might be interesting to see to what extent black youth in Britain feel the same about their white counterparts.

Young people's interests, expectations, priorities, and concerns are much the same as they have been for many generations — taking on various adult roles of responsibility, having personal relationships, doing well at school, getting a job. Many of the questions on wider political, economic, and intergroup affairs drew not particularly unusual, extreme, or surprising answers.

Of course, there are many other important issues that were not addressed in our questionnaire. Although we attempted to be comprehensive in our coverage, lack of space and time meant that some issues had to be omitted while others had to be dealt with in a very limited number of questions. Nevertheless, we believe we have provided a fairly detailed insight into the anatomy of adolescence beliefs.

COMPARATIVE ISSUES

Market and opinion researchers frequently 'break down' their results in terms of sex, age, and class, meaning that they analyse their responses looking at the differences between the sexes, different age groups, and different social classes, Many attitudes, beliefs, and behaviours are a function of these three major demographic variables.

With all of the topics examined in this study we broke the data down in terms of age, sex, and class but also in terms of intended vote (from left- to right-wing) and religion. We analysed every question in terms of these five different factors in order to see if there were any major differences. Where there were a number of major, statistically significant differences in responses to questions in one area, they were reported in the tables. Thus, if we reported on sex and age differences, the implication was that there were no, or few, class, religion, or political preference differences.

A casual glance at the tables in the preceding chapters show *no* religion or vote breakdowns, a few class differences, but a fairly large number of sex and age differences. There may be a number of reasons why class, political preference, or religious differences did not show up many important differences. The most obvious answer may be that religious beliefs, political preferences, and social class do not relate to the sort of questions posed in this study. More probably it may be that these factors only become important as people get older and that, whereas adult social class or political preference are powerful determinants of social attitudes, they are much less important in adolescence. Third, it is possible that the way in which these three factors were measured means that any differences that did exist did not show up. It is notoriously difficult to measure things like social class or political preference since different ways of defining or measuring these may yield substantially different results.

Of these three possible reasons it is very likely that the second is most important. That is, it is not that social class, religious, or political preference factors do not relate to social attitudes but that they do so more systematically and powerfully as people get older. Certainly, political opinions are not as well formed in adolescence as are religious beliefs. Furthermore, to classify social class among young people it is most unusual to use parental occupation which may be immediately reported and more importantly may not indicate the social class in which young people may find themselves in their adulthood.

There were, however, very many age and sex differences. It is difficult to make general statements about the nature of these differences except on a somewhat glib level. The sex differences did show an interesting and a consistent pattern overall on many topics, particularly in issues of sexual, racial, and political *equality*, females appeared to be more liberal and less conservative than males. The results tended to be similar to those of other studies looking at sex differences in young people: females tend to describe themselves more often as liberal or radical, and less often as conservative, than males; females are more ideologically homogeneous than males and express less general and political/economic conservatism in their attitudes; females are more negative towards racism, punitiveness, and social inequality, but are more positive towards religion compared with males. Elsewhere, females and males seem quite similar in their social attitudes.

There were also a large number of age differences. Although the pattern was not always linear, with the youngest group agreeing least or most, then the middle group, followed by the oldest group, the results, more often than not, were linear as opposed to curvilinear. What was most often the trend was not that older adolescents were more sceptical, more knowledgeable, and less optimistic. Particularly with regard to issues of equality, older adolescents seemed less supportive than the youngest group. They also appeared to be more pessimistic about the future, particularly with respect to jobs, a safer world, and the environment. These results were not surprising. Indeed, given that the youngest people among our respondents were 10 years old and the oldest in their early twenties (the vast majority being between 13 and 18 years old), it is perhaps surprising that there were not more significant age differences. Adolescence is frequently characterized by a period of continual and major change, hence one might expect substantial changes in attitudes to all sorts of things. Certainly, the results reported in this book suggest that this is only true of particular issues, usually those close to the experience of young people.

Finally, for some of the questions on which we have data, comparisons can be made with opinions held by British adults. This was particularly the case with items concerned with the governance of Britain reported in chapter 3. Whereas there were important differences between adults and adolescents, there was less evidence of difference than of similarity. Our adolescents seemed less in favour of the monarchy, less in favour of nuclear weapons, more favourably disposed to the trade unions, more ready to break the law than adults: in short, less conservative. But like adults they believed trade unions had too much power and were overall in favour of capital punishment. Yet both adults and adolescents had very similar views on how well or badly run British institutions were and what the major problems facing Britain are. All in all there seemed more similarity than difference.

Although we collected data from young people from all parts of Great Britain — England, Northern Ireland, Scotland, and Wales — we did not look for regional differences. This may have yielded some very interesting findings but was beyond the scope of this research.

Perhaps the most important comparative data are those gathered *over time*. It is not much more than a decade before the end of both the century and the millennium. In that time many changes are anticipated and many will no doubt occur. It will be most interesting to examine the attitudes, beliefs, values, and self-reported behaviours of young people, in Britain and other countries, as that date approaches.

REFERENCES

Aaro, L.E., Wold B., Kannas, L., and Rimpola, M. (1986) 'Health behaviour in schoolchildren: a WHO cross-national survey', *Health Promotion* 1 (1): 17–33.

Adelson, J. (1971) 'The political imaginations of the young adolescent', *Daedalus* Fall: 1013–44.

Adorno, T.W., Frenkel-Brunswick, E., Levinson, D.J., and Sanford, R.N. (1950) *The Authoritarian Personality*, New York: Harper,

Airey, C. (1984) 'Social and moral values', in R. Jowell and C. Airey (eds) *British Social Attitudes: The 1984 Report*, Aldershot: Gower.

Airey, C. and Brook, L. (1986) 'Interim report: social and moral issues', in R. Jowell, S. Witherspoon, and L. Brook (eds) *British Social Attitudes: The 1986 Report*, Aldershot: Gower.

Ajzen, I. and Fishbein, M. (1977) 'Attitude-behaviour relations: a theoretical analysis and review of empirical research', *Psychological Bulletin* 84: 888–918.

Argyle, M. and Henderson, M. (1985) *The Anatomy of Relationships*, London: Heinemann.

Aries, P. (1962) *Centuries of Childhood: A Social History of Family Life*, translated by R. Baldrick, New York: Vintage Books.

Bagley, C. and Verma, G. (1973) 'Inter-ethnic attitudes and behaviour in British multi-racial schools', in C. Bagley and G. Verma (eds) *Race and Education Across Cultures*, London: Heinemann.

Banks, M. and Jackson, P. (1982) 'Unemployment and risk of minor psychiatric disorder in young people: cross-sectional and longitudinal evidence', *Psychological Medicine* 12: 789–98.

Barton, M. (1984) 'Race, prejudice and education: changing approaches', *New Community* 11: 373–80.

Barzini, L. (1983) *The Impossible Europeans*, London: Weidenfeld.

Bell, C.G. (ed.) (1973) *Growth and Change: A Reader in Political Socialisation*, Encino, CA: Dickinson.

Berkowitz, C. and Lutterman, K. (1968) 'The traditionally socially responsible personality', *Public Opinion Quarterly* 32: 160–85.

Blood, M. (1969) 'Work values and job satisfaction', *Journal of Applied Psychology* 53: 456–9.

Bloom, L. (1972) *The Social Psychology of Race Relations*, London: Allen & Unwin.

Blumler, J. (1974) 'Does mass political ignorance matter?', *Teaching Politics* 3: 59–65.

Boddewyn, J.J. (1986) *Why Do Juveniles Start Smoking?*, New York: International Advertising Association.

British Broadcasting Corporation (1977) *Annual Review of Audience Research Findings*, London: BBC.

Chester, M. (1976) 'Contemporary sociological theories of racism', in P. Katz (ed.) *Towards the Elimination of Racism*, New York: Pergamon.

Christiansen, B. (1959) *Attitudes towards Foreign Affairs as a Function of Personality*, Oslo: Oslo University Press.

Cochrane, R. and Billig, M. (1982) 'Extremism of the centre', *New Society* May: 291–3.

Darcy, J. (1978) 'Education about unemployment: a reflective element', *Oxford Review of Education* 4: 289–94.

Dayton, C. (1981) 'The young person's job search: insights from a study', *Journal of Counselling Psychology* 20: 321–33.

Dennis, J. and McCrone, D. (1970) 'The adult development of political party identification in Western democracies', *Comparative Political Studies* 3: 243–63.

De Vito, A. J., Bogdanowitz, J., and Reznikoff, M. (1982) 'Actual and intended health-related information seeking and health locus of control', *Journal of Personality Assessment* 46: 63–9.

Dobbs, J. and Marsh, A. (1985) *Smoking Among Secondary School Children in 1984*, an enquiry carried out for the Department of Health and Social Security, the Welsh Office of Population Censuses and Surveys, Social Survey Division.

Donnell, K. (1979) *Family Information*, London: HMSO.

Dowse, R. and Hughes, J. (1971) 'Girls, boys and politics', *British Journal of Sociology* 22: 53–7.

Driver, M. (1963) *Conceptual Structure and Group Processes in an Inter-Nation Simulation*, Princeton, NJ: Education Testing Service.

Duncan, O.D., Schuman, H., and Duncan, B. (1973) *Social Change in a Metropolitan Community*, New York: Russell Sage Foundation.

Egan, O. and Nugent, J. (1983) 'Adolescent conceptions of the homeland: a cross-cultural study', *Journal of Youth and Adolescence* 12: 185–201.

Eisenberg-Berg, N. (1979) 'Relationships of prosocial moral reasoning to political liberalism and intelligence', *Developmental Psychology* 15: 87–9.

Ekehammar, B. (1985) 'Sex differences in socio-political attitudes revisited', *Educational Studies* 11: 3–9.

Feather, N. (1977) 'Generation and sex differences in Conservatism', *Australian Psychologist* 12: 76–82.

Figueroa, P. and Swat, L. (1986) 'Teachers' and pupils' racist and ethnocentric frames of reference: a case study', *New Community* 13: 40–51.

Forgas, J. and O'Driscoll, M. (1985) 'Cross-cultural and demographic difference in the perception of nations', *Journal of Cross Cultural Psychology*.

Furnham, A. (1984a) 'The Protestant work ethic, voting behaviour and attitudes to trade unions', *Political Studies* 32: 420–36.

Furnham, A. (1984b) 'Getting a job: school-leavers' perceptions of employment prospects', *British Journal of Educational Psychology* 54: 293–305.

Furnham, A. (1985a) 'Adolescents' socio-political attitudes: a study of sex and national differences', *Political Psychology* 6: 621–36.

Furnham, A. (1985b) 'Just world beliefs in an unjust society: a cross-cultural comparison', *European Journal of Social Psychology* 15.

Furnham, A. (1985c) 'Youth unemployment: a review of the literature', *Journal of Adolescence* 5: 109–24.

Furnham, A. (1986) 'Response bias, social desirability and dissimulation', *Personality and Individual Differences* 7: 385–400.

Furnham, A. (1988) *The Work Ethic: The Psychology of Work Beliefs and Values*, London: Methuen.

Furnham, A. and Gunter, B. (1983) 'Political knowledge and awareness in adolescence', *Journal of Adolescence* 6: 373–85.

Furnham, A. and Lewis, A. (1986) *The Economic Mind: The Social Psychology of Economic Behaviour*, Brighton: Wheatsheaf.

Furnham, A., Johnson, C., and Rawls, R. (1985) 'The determinants of beliefs in human nature', *Personality and Individual Differences* 6: 675–84.

Garofalo, J. and Laub, J. (1981) 'The fear of crime: broadcasting over perspective', *Victimology: An International Journal* 3: 242–53.

Gillies, D., Elwood, J.M., Pearson, J.C.G., and Cust, G. (1987) 'An adolescent smoking survey in Trent, and its contribution to health promotion', *Health Education Journal* 43 (1): 19–22.

Greenstein, F. (1961) 'Sex-related political differences in childhood', *Journal of Politics* 21: 353–71.

Gunter, B. and Greenberg, B. (1986) 'Media use', *Times Educational Supplement* October.

Haldane, I.R. (1978) 'Who and what is religious broadcasting for?' *Independent Broadcasting* 13–16.

Heald, G. and Wybrow, R.J. (1986) *The Gallup Survey of Britain*, London: Croom Helm.

Her Majesty's Stationery Office (1983) *Young People in the 80s: A Survey*, London: HMSO.

Hess, R. and Torney, J. (1967) *The Development of Political Attitudes in Children*, Chicago: Aldine.

Hewstone, M. (1986) *Understanding Attitudes to the European Community*, Cambridge: Cambridge University Press.

Himmelweit, H. and Swift, B. (1971) *Social and Personality Factors in the*

Development of Adult Attitudes Towards Self and Society, London: SSRC Report.

Himmelweit, H., Humphreys, P., Jaeger, M., and Katz, M. (1981) *How Voters Decide*, London: Academic Press.

Hood, E., Lindsay, W., and Brooks, N. (1982) 'Interview training with adolescents', *Behaviour Research and Therapy* 20: 581-92.

Hough, M. and Mayhew, P. (1985) *Taking Account of Crime: Key Findings from the 1984 British Crime Survey*, London: HMSO.

Independent Broadcasting Authority (1987) *Attitudes to Broadcasting*, London: IBA.

Independent Television Authority (1970) *Religion in Britain and Northern Ireland: A Survey of Popular Attitudes*, London: ITA.

Inhelder, B. and Piaget, J. (1958) *The Growth of Logical Thinking from Childhood to Adolescence*, New York: Basic Books.

Jackson, P., Stafford, E., Banks, M., and Warr, P. (1983) 'Unemployment and psychological distress in young people: the moderating role of employment commitment', *Journal of Applied Psychology* 68: 525-35.

Jaros, D. and Grant, L. (1974) *Political Behaviour: Choices and Perspectives*, Oxford: Blackwell.

Jennings, M. and Niemi, R. (1971) 'The division of political labor between fathers and mothers', *American Political Science Review* 65: 64-82.

Jowell, R. and Airey, C. (eds) (1984) *British Social Attitudes: The 1984 Report*, Aldershot: Gower.

Jowell, R. and Witherspoon, S. (eds) (1985) *British Social Attitudes: The 1985 Report*, Aldershot: Gower.

Jowell, R., Witherspoon, S., and Brook, C. (eds) (1986) *British Social Attitudes: The 1986 Report*, Aldershot: Gower.

Katz, P. (1976) 'The acquisition of racial attitudes in children', in P. Katz (ed.) *Towards the Elimination of Racism*, New York: Pergamon.

King, J. (1982) 'The patient's dilemma', *New Society* March: 388-9.

Landis, J.T. (1960) 'The trauma of children when parents divorce', *Marriage and Family Living* 22: 7-13.

Langton, K. (1969) *Political Socialization*, New York: Oxford University Press.

Lau, R.R. (1982) 'Origins of health locus of control beliefs', *Journal of Personality and Social Psychology* 42: 322-34.

Lerner, M.J., Miller, D.T., and Holmes, J.G. (1970) 'Deserving and the emergence of forms of justice', in L. Berkowitz and E. Walster (eds) *Advances in Experimental Social Psychology*, New York: Academic Press.

Makeham, P. (1980) *Youth Unemployment: An Examination of Youth Unemployment Using National Statistics*, London: Department of Employment.

Mussen, P., Sullivan, L., and Eisenberg-Berg, N. (1977) 'Changes in political-economic attitudes during adolescence', *Journal of Genetic Psychology* 140: 64-76.

Muuss, R.E. (1970) 'Adolescent development and the secular trend', *Adolescence* 5: 267–86.

Nelson, E.A., Eisenberg-Berg, N., and Carroll, J.L. (1982) 'The structure of adolescents' attitudes towards law and crime', *Journal of Genetic Psychology* 140: 47–58.

Niemi, R.G. (1973) 'Political socialisation', in J.H. Knutson (ed.) *Handbook of Political Psychology*, San Francisco, CA: Jossey-Bass.

Oppenheim, A. (1966) *Questionnaire Measurement and Design*, London: Heinemann.

Oppenheim, A. and Torney, J. (1974) *The Measurement of Children's Attitudes in Different Nations*, Stockholm: Almquist da Wiksell International.

Poole, M. (1983) *Youth: Expectations and Transitions*, Melbourne: Routledge.

Ramprakash, D. (1986) *Social Trends No. 16*, London: HMSO.

Ray, J. (1980) 'Authoritarianism in California 30 years later — with some cross-cultural comparisons', *Journal of Social Psychology* 111: 9–17.

Ray, J. (1983) 'Is Britain an authoritarian society?', in V. Kool and J. Ray (eds) *Authoritarianism Across Cultures*, Bombay: Himalaya Press.

Ray, J. (1984) 'Achievement motivation as a source of racism, conservatism and authoritarianism', *Journal of Social Psychology* 122: 163–4.

Roper Organization (1983) *Trends in Attitudes Towards Television and Other Media: A Twenty-Year Review*, New York: Television Information Office.

Sampson, D. and Smith, H. (1957) 'A scale to measure world-minded attitudes', *Journal of Social Psychology* 45: 99–106.

Sawyer, J. (1967) 'Dimensions of nations: size, wealth and politics', *American Journal of Sociology* 73: 145–72.

Sharma, S. (1980) 'Perceptions of political institutions among Asian and English adolescents in Britain', *New Community* 6: 240–7.

Sidanius, J. and Ekehammar, B. (1980) 'Sex-related differences in socio-political ideology', *Scandinavian Journal of Psychology* 21: 17–26.

Sidanius, J., Ekehammar, B., and Ross, M. (1979) 'Comparisons of socio-political attitudes between two democratic societies', *International Journal of Psychology* 14: 225–40.

Simmons, C. and Wade, W. (1984) *I Like to Say . . . What I Think: A Study of the Attitudes, Values and Beliefs of Young People Today*, London: Kogan Page.

Stevens, O. (1982) *Children Talking Politics*, Oxford: Martin Robertson.

Stradling, R. (1977) *The Political Awareness of the School Leavers*, London: Hansard Society.

Strickland, B.R. (1978) 'Internal-external expectancies and health-related behaviours', *Journal of Consulting and Clinical Psychology* 46: 1192–211.

Wallston, B. S., Wallston, K. A., Kaplan, G.B., and Maides, S.A. (1976) 'Development and validation of health locus of control (HLC) scale', *Journal of Consulting and Clinical Psychology* 44: 580–5.

Walvin, J. (1984) *Passage to Britain*, Harmondsworth: Penguin.

Watkins, L. and Worcester, R. (1986) *Private Opinions Public Polls*, London: Thames & Hudson.

Watts, A. (1978) 'The implications for school leavers: unemployment for careers education in schools', *Journal of Curriculum Studies* 3: 233–50.

Webb, N. and Wybrow, R. (eds) (1981) *The Gallup Report*, Reading: Sphere.

Wish, M., Deutsch, M., and Brener, L. (1970) 'Differences in conceptual structures of nations: an exploratory study', *Journal of Personality and Social Psychology* 16: 361–73.

Witherspoon, S. (1985) 'Sex roles and gender issues', in R. Jowell and S. Witherspoon (eds) *British Social Attitudes: The 1985 Report*, Aldershot: Gower.

Wober, M. (1981) 'British attitudes towards Europe: an exploration of their inner structure', *British Journal of Social Psychology* 20: 181–8.

Wober, M. (1986) 'Television and viewers' involvement in the 1984 European Parliamentary Election', *European Journal of Communication*.

Young, K. (1985) 'Local government and the environment', in R. Jowell and S. Witherspoon (eds) *British Social Attitudes: The 1985 Report*, Aldershot: Gower.

Young, K. (1986) 'A green and pleasant land', in R. Jowell, S. Witherspoon, and L. Brook (eds) *British Social Attitudes: The 1986 Report*, Aldershot: Gower.

Zillmann, D. and Wakshlag, J. (1985) 'Fear of victimization and the appeal of crime drama', in D. Zillmann and J. Bryant (eds) *Selective Exposure to Communication*, Hillsdale, NJ: Lawrence Erlbaum Associates.

INDEX